Mama's Torah

The Role of Women

Batya Ruth Wootten

Mama's Torah: The Role of Women

by Batya Ruth Wootten

Cover design by Tim Hall, John Diffenderfer, and Batya Wootten. Painting, "Jesus as a Little Child" by Del Parson. Used by permission. Del Parson Studio, Cedar City, UT 84720. www.delparson.com

Published by: Key of David Publishing, PO Box 700217, Saint Cloud, FL 34770 407.344.7700.
www.keyofdavidpublishing.com

Distributed by: Messianic Israel Ministries, PO Box 3263, Lebanon TN 37088 800.829.8777
www.mim.net

Printed in the United States of America.
All quotations used by permission.

Unless otherwise noted, Scripture quotations are from the *New American Standard Bible* (NASB), © 1995, The Lockman Foundation, published by Holman Bible Publishers, Nashville; and the *New New American Standard Bible*, Quick Verse for Windows, © 1992-1999, Craig Rairdon and Parsons Technology.
Verses marked KJV are from the *King James Version* Bible.
Verses marked NRSV are from *The New Revised Standard Version With Apocrypha*, © 1998 by Electronic Edition STEP Files, Parsons Technology, Inc. Cedar Rapids, Iowa.
Verses marked NIV are from the *New International Version*, © 1995 by The International Bible Society, published by Zondervan Publishing House, Grand Rapids.
Verses marked TAB are from *The Amplified Bible*, © 1994 by the Zondervan Publishing House, Grand Rapids.

Note: To emphasize some Scriptures, italics or an alternate word choice has been used, especially for the names of the Father and Son. Also, brackets [] indicate text added by the author.

ISBN 1-886987-20-3

Acknowledgments

My deepest thanks go to those who helped to critique, and to proofread, this work. I especially want to thank Hollisa Alewine, Michele Libin, and John Conrad. Thanks also to Del Parson, who generously allowed us to reproduce his fine artwork on the front cover. And to my husband, Angus, who always encourages me in my writings.

Finally, I want to thank those in whose research footsteps I have followed. Many have labored long and hard to help establish the true scriptural role of women. I pray that this book will add further insight to the great works of those who have gone before me.

Batya Wootten
Saint Cloud, FL

"Hear, my son, your father's instruction
and do not forsake your mother's _torah_."
"Keep your father's commands
and do not forsake your mother's _torah_.
Bind them upon your heart forever;
fasten them around your neck.
When you walk they will guide you;
when you sleep, they will watch over you;
when you awake, they will speak to you"
(Proverbs 1:8; 6:20-22).

תּוֹרָה

Torah

- Law, direction, instruction (human or divine)
- Body of prophetic teaching
- Instruction in Messianic age

The Almighty says that He loved Abraham because he kept His "laws," or "Torah" (Genesis 26:5).

Abraham kept the *spirit* of the Father's torah before the letter of it was given to Moses.

Everyone who wants to be a success should likewise look to our Father's precepts for guidance. For Moses said of them, "Keep and do them, for that is your wisdom and your understanding in the sight of the peoples who will hear all these statutes and say, 'Surely this great nation is a wise and understanding people'" (Deuteronomy 4:5-6).

The Psalmist said, "How blessed are those whose way is blameless, who walk in the law of the Lord. How blessed are those who observe His testimonies, who seek Him with all their heart. They also do no unrighteousness; they walk in His ways....Oh that my ways may be established to keep Thy statutes! Then I shall not be ashamed" (Psalm 119:1-6).

As New Covenant Believers, we are saved by grace, not by works—by the shed blood of our Messiah, and by the word of our testimony.

It is with this understanding of all that our Messiah has done for us, and of the wise and simple faith of our forefather, Abraham, that we speak of "honoring the wisdom of Torah."

Ephraim —

Ephraim is the given name of
Joseph's second son.
It means "doubly fruitful."
The name was also used to describe the
Ten Tribes of the Northern Kingdom,
who were known as the Kingdom of Israel.

Ephraimite —

A name used to describe those of the
Northern Kingdom of Israel
(as opposed to the
Southern Kingdom of Judah).
These Ten Tribes eventually lost their identity
some time after they were exiled by the
Assyrians around 722 BC.
It likewise describes Israelites, or Hebrews,
from the natural seed of Jacob,
specifically those referred to as the
"Ten Lost Tribes."
It also is used to describe the
"companions" who sojourn with them.
In this work, this generic term is broadly used
to speak of the non-Jewish
Believers in the Messiah of Israel
(Genesis 41:52; 2 Kings 17:34;
1 Kings 12:21 Ezekiel 37:15-28).

Contents

• Introduction

Chapters

Introduction

Scripture speaks of a "period of restoration of *all things* about which God spoke by the mouth of His holy prophets..." (Acts 3:20-21).

"All things" includes women.

Surely believing women need to be restored to the place the Almighty planned for them when He created them in His image. He "created man in His own image, in the image of God He created him; male and female He created them" (Genesis 1:27).

Woman too was created in the image of the Holy One, and many women long to be restored to that rightful place. They want to truly mirror what the Father had in mind when He created them. As godly women they do not want to go beyond that perfect image, nor to fall short of all that Abba had in mind when He began to fashion a certain rib.

And yet...

Many women feel frustrated about the place they are, and are not, given in the believing community. They desperately want to know, and to walk in, the Father's truth as outlined for them.

This book is written with the prayer that it might help represent that truth, and help us better walk in that truth as we discern what the Father has in mind for us at this time in history.

It also is written especially to women who desire to return to their Hebraic roots, to those of the Messianic faith. It issues a clarion call for believing women to arise. It is a call sent forth to those who love the truth of the Scriptures—Genesis to Revelation.

My husband, Angus, and I have labored long and hard in the Messianic field. We have sought to help the Body to understand about "both the houses of Israel" (Isaiah 8:14).

We write with an understanding about all Israel—Ephraim and Judah—as part of our foundation.

For decades we have taught about *the "melo hagoyim,"* meaning "the fullness of Gentiles" that Jacob prophesied would come from Joseph's son, Ephraim (Genesis 48:19; Romans 11:25).

We have taught in detail about the Northern and Southern Kingdoms of Israel, and about how the Father is now making the two, and their companions, "one stick in His hand" (Ezekiel 37:15-28).

People the world over are now seeing this truth. Believers [a] are returning to their Hebraic roots in droves. They are learning that Jesus' given name in Hebrew is Yeshua,[b] that He is the Messiah of all Israel, and that He is the King of all twelve tribes.

---

a We use *Believer* to describe those purchased by Messiah Yeshua's blood, rather than *Christian,* because the latter title is often misused (see Mat 7:23; 1 Cor 6:20; 1 Pet 1:17-19).

b *Yeshua* (ישוע) is the Messiah's given Hebrew name, it means "Salvation" (Mat 1:21). When transliterated into Greek, due to linguistic differences, *Yeshua* became *Iesous* (Ιησους). In Old English, "Iesous" was then rendered "Iesus" (pronounced *Yesus*), and was spelled with a beginning letter "J," which at the time had a "Y" sound. Later the "J" came to have a harder sound, and it came to be pronounced as "Jesus." Since this name is the result of linguistic differences, we prefer to use the Messiah's given Hebrew/Aramaic Name, Yeshua.

They also are beginning to be drawn to the eternal truths of Torah.

Teachings about Torah and the Two Houses of Israel are exploding all over the literary map. Then again, the Messianic movement seems to be stuck in a proverbial "rut." In some ways it is even guilty of fostering a certain "falling away" from the Messiah.

This is occurring because, if we teach about Israel but do not include all Israel, Jewish and non-Jewish Believers alike, we do a disservice to those whom we exclude. We cut them off from their hope of being part of the chosen people of the Holy One of Israel (Deuteronomy 7:6; 1 Peter 1:1; 2:9-10).

In this special time when our Father is seeking to bring His children together, some have unfairly and excessively elevated the teachings of Judaism, while at the same time unfairly demeaning those of Christianity. Thus, we are hemorrhaging Believers. Some are walking away from faith in our divine Messiah and converting to Judaism.

Women have a role to play in helping to bring our ship back on course in this hour. So does a true move of the *Ruach HaKodesh*, the Holy Spirit. For if we teach about *Torah*, or Abba's *Loving Instructions* to His people, yet do not include the One destined to write the Torah on our hearts, Torah will never be known in its fullness (Jeremiah 31:31-33).

To have a Hebraic renaissance wherein Believers are truly interested in their Hebraic Roots, to have a revival based on the scriptural truths of our fore-fathers, we must have a true move of the *Ruach HaKodesh*.

The move of the Holy One that we seek in these last day will not happen based on Torah knowledge or the might of men, but by the power of YHVH's (God's) Holy Spirit:

"This is the word of the Lord [YHVH]... 'Not by might nor by power, but by My Spirit,' says YHVH of hosts" (Zechariah 4:6).

Again, if we teach about Torah, yet do not release the vessels of mercy destined to help lay its foundation, we build our house on shifting sand. For this reason and more, the Messianic movement desperately needs to acknowledge the truth about the role of women.

The coming move of the Holy One is especially geared toward teaching Israel to return to the ancient paths, to the spirit of His principles.

"Thus says YHVH, 'Stand by the ways and see and ask for the ancient paths, where the good way is, and walk in it; and you will find rest for your souls." And, "Look to Abraham your father and to Sarah who gave birth to you in pain; when he was but one I called him, then I blessed him and multiplied him'" (Jeremiah 6:16; Isaiah 51:2).

Adherents of the Messianic movement desire to see the Torah of our forefathers restored to its rightful place. They want to see its wisdom properly honored. However, the truths of Torah will never be properly taught until the women among us are encouraged to walk in their proper role. For Abba long ago ordained that a true Torah-honoring lifestyle would begin with the mothers of Israel.

Women who love the Almighty are His nurturing vessels of mercy. They need to be released in this hour. They need to be fully restored to all that the Father had in mind when He created them.

This book is dedicated to that restoration.

Batya Ruth Wootten

One

The Restoration of All Things

*W*e are closer to the end than any generation that has gone before us. However, there are certain things that must happen before our Messiah's return, and one very important aspect of our restoration has to do with woman...

Women often are not appreciated for the unique creatures they were created to be.

Their special giftings and talents are thus lost to the Body of Messiah—which in turn suffers because it does not really hear from the women among them.

To help release the captives, to help them become the spiritual deliverers they were created to be, we will examine the call and role of women as outlined in the Old and New Covenants.

Beginning at the Book of Beginnings, or Genesis, we see that in the cool of the evening, the Almighty used to walk and talk with man. Then we fell, and intimate conversation with our Creator was thereafter hindered.

That is, until the coming of Jesus, or Yeshua, the blessed Messiah of Israel.

Yeshua came to restore that which was lost, to restore mankind. That restoration includes woman, for she too is of "man" (Luke 19:10; Genesis 1:27).

The Book of Acts tells us to repent and return to the Almighty, that times of refreshing might come. It also tells us that our Messiah has been received into the heavenlies, there to remain until "the period of restoration of all things about which God spoke by the mouth of His holy prophets..." (Acts 3:19-21).

Among the things that must be restored is the whole house of Israel: "'Behold, days are coming,' declares YHVH, 'when I will restore the fortunes of My people Israel *and* Judah....I will also bring them back to the land that I gave to their forefathers and they will possess it'" (Jeremiah 30:3-4).

The Holy One has promised to save both Judah and Israel. When they come together, they will return to Zion, and will thereafter call Zion "The City of Truth" (Zechariah 8:3,7,13).

Ezekiel describes this reunited Israel as two sticks, one symbolizing the house of Judah and their companions, the other signifying the house of Joseph/Ephraim and their companions. He tells us that the

God of Israel will make these two houses "one stick" in His hand.

Ezekiel gives three hallmarks that identify this restored Israel:

- They become one nation in the Land
- They have one King, Yeshua
- They no longer defile themselves with *any* of their sins, transgressions, or idols (Ezekiel 37:22-26).

ONE STICK IN HIS HAND

(←"One Stick" print by Crystal Lenhart: www.mim.net.)

These and many other important prophecies about restored Israel have not yet been fulfilled.[1]   The principle reason is that a true move of the Holy Spirit, preaching true Torah, and the release of women, has much to do with Israel's full restoration.

Those who feel drawn to "Israel" often are aware of the Messianic call to return to Torah. However, many are likewise aware of the excesses put forth by some who are involved in that call.

Nonetheless, the Father's plan to ultimately have His law written on the hearts of His people continues to be valid. It even lies at the heart of His promised New Covenant:

"'Behold, days are coming,' declares YHVH,' when I will make a new covenant with the house of Israel and with the house of Judah, not like the covenant which I made with their fathers...which they broke, although I was a husband to them,' declares YHVH. 'But this is the covenant which I will make with the house of Israel after those days,' declares YHVH, 'I will put My law within them and on their heart I will write it; and I will be their God, and they shall be My people" (Jeremiah 31:31-33).

A "Better" Covenant?

The New Covenant is said to be a "better covenant" (Hebrews 7:22).[2]   However, in some circles, the position of women does not appear to be any better than it was before the coming of Messiah.

In ancient Greco-Roman circles, and even in the Jewish circles of that time, women were, at best, to be seen, but never heard. To this day, the idea that

1 See the Restored Israel Hallmarks Chart in the Study Helps section; also see, "Hallmarks of Restored Israel", *Who is Israel?*, by Batya Wootten. Key of David. Saint Cloud, FL. 2003.
2 This is the New Covenant established by Messiah Yeshua. See Luke 22:20; 1 Cor 11:25; Heb 7:22; 8:6-13; 9:15; 12:24.

women are to be silenced persists in many congregations, Christian and Jewish alike.

The truth is that women today should have no more, nor less, positions than did their sisters in the Old and New Covenants. Therefore, we will first examine these Covenants, and then explore the Father's latter day call on the women of restored Israel.

This book assumes that the full restoration of women is inextricably linked to the full restoration of all Israel, because a true Abrahamic-type Torah of the heart plays a crucial role in that restoration.

It also assumes that women need to, are even destined to, arise in this hour.

We're Different

In addition, we presume that women are different from men, and that they were deliberately created that way so that they might serve a divine purpose.

- Woman is the only created being not taken directly from the ground.
- Woman is highly intuitive.
- Woman tends to be more "spiritually attuned" to the world around her than her male counterpart, who tends to be more logically oriented.
- Woman is the one who nurtures the children, while her husband tends to be the one who corrects them.

As we will see, these traits have much to do with establishing right order among all of the Father's people.

We will now briefly examine woman's call to be a "wife" to her husband.

Two

A Divine Radar System

*W*oman was created to be a wife to her man (Genesis 2:24). But what does it mean to be a good wife? Does it mean that we must quietly submit to everything our husbands tell us?

In one way, that would be the easy way out.

Having to say something to your mate when you know he will not like what you are going to say is not without difficulty. Being silent might be easier.

If only we were equipped that way.

But we're not. Instead, women were created to be a type of "Divine Radar System," ever giving off warning signals to their mates.

"Honey, that man is not your friend," says the wife.

"What do you mean?" the irritated husband asks.

"I don't exactly know," replies the wife. "I just know that you should not do business with him. I get a bad feeling when I'm around him."

"So what am I to do? I need his business. His account could make a bit difference to me," he says.

"I don't know" she repeats, "I just get a bad feeling..."

Situations like this occur every day with husbands and wives. The wife is trying to warn her husband about what she senses concerning the businessman she distrusts, but she cannot give her husband clear direction as to what he should do about the situation, for she cannot give him more nor less than what she actually feels she is "getting in the spirit."

Should the husband refuse to do business with the man based solely on his wife's input?

Probably not. Instead, he needs to filter her input through his logical mind, take the matter to the Lord in prayer, and then make his decision.

Should the wife not give her advice since it is incomplete?

No. She must transmit what she has received.

That is her job.

Blip, Blip, Blip...

Just as a radar system serves to warn planes of impending danger, so woman was created to warn her husband of impending danger.

Women tend to be "spirit beings." Like a radar system, women are very "intuitive."

Women were especially created to pick up signals and to then convey them to their beloved husbands.

However, this service is sometimes received about as warmly as the continual and annoying "Blip, blip, blip" sound associated with a real radar system.

Regardless of how it is received, woman must continue to send forth her signals.

To do anything less is to fail at her assignment.

On the other hand, a good wife must be careful with her "Blip, blip, blips," lest they sound to her man like "Drip, drip, drip." For the Word warns us that "A quarrelsome wife is like a constant dripping" (Proverbs 19:13, NIV).

A woman must tell her man what she senses in the spirit, and if he does not listen, then she must tell him again. If he still doesn't listen, with all due respect, she must then tell him that she told him, that he didn't listen, and so she had to tell him again. And if he still doesn't listen, she must tell him again, and again, and again...

Silence would be easier. But a good wife cares about the well-being of her husband, so she persists.

However, she must always do so with the utmost respect for him. "The wife must see to it that she respects her husband" (Ephesians 5:33).

Even when the husband's behavior is not what it should be, the wife needs to respect the office that he holds. She needs to honor the Father's divine order, even if the man she is married to is being difficult.

At the same time, it goes without saying that this axiom would not hold true if a husband were being abusive, because a marriage license is not a license to abuse.

Granted, it is difficult for woman to trust in her "head" when she feels like the head does not know where it is going, but trust she must.

At such times she especially needs to come to her husband's aid in intercessory prayer. She can even pray openly for her mate, but never let it be that the prayer is full of "scripture bullets" with which she tries to shoot him.

Prayers for one's mate should always be uplifting and encouraging. For example:

"Father, I thank you for my husband and ask that you please grant him the gift of wisdom, and that you give it to him in abundance."

"Abba, please help my husband to know the direction in which we should go as a family. Speak to him in the night, even as he sleeps."

"Father, please give my husband the gift of discernment of spirits that he might better understand the motives of those who work with him."

"Abba, please help my husband to walk in a way that causes him to be respected in the gates. Help him to be a man who brings honor to Your Name."

"Abba, please open up the windows of Heaven and bless my husband..."

Three

Sails and Anchors

*I*n the "Good Ship Marriage," we find a picture of the different roles of husband and wife.

In a marriage, the woman can be likened to the sail, and the man to the anchor.

Woman tends to be more intuitive and is often the first to "catch the wind of the Spirit." And when all is well, a sail can carry the ship to wonderful, far away, dreamy places.

Women often catch the wind and direction of the spirit before their husbands even know that the wind is blowing. So it is that wives sometimes want to run in a new direction, but their beloved "anchor" holds them back. He won't go along for the ride.

On the down side, sails have the capacity to catch a bad wind, and to run the ship aground.

Women can be intuitive, yet they can be deceived, and they are best served when their intuitive gleanings are sifted through the filter that is man's logic. So it is that sails and anchors go well together.

The Anchor

Husbands are like anchors. They tend to be steady and often are the ones who stay the marital ship in a storm.

But on the other hand...

Being anchored to one place when one feels restless can be boring and frustrating.

It also can prove to be a real test of woman's faithfulness.

As women, when we sense that something wonderful in the spirit is happening "over there," and we want to join in, our mates can remind us of an unmovable stick in the mud.

This in turn can be a true test for the wives.

Will you honor the Father's plan? Will you respect your husband's wishes? "For this is the way the holy women of the past who put their hope in God used to make themselves beautiful. They were submissive to their own husbands, like Sarah, who obeyed Abraham and called him her master. You are her daughters if you do what is right and do not give way to fear" (1 Peter 3:5-6, NIV).

Sarah and Rebekah

This is not to say that women are always to "obey" every word that their husbands speak.

When Sarah knew what had to be done with Hagar and Ishmael, and Abraham did not, the Holy One said to Abraham, "Listen to whatever Sarah tells you" (Genesis 21:12, NIV).

Rebekah similarly understood the Father's plan when Isaac did not. (Had it not been for her intervention, perhaps Esau, and not Jacob, would have inherited his father's blessing [Genesis 27:1-10].)

Mutual Respect

In a similar fashion, husbands are instructed to "be considerate as you live with your wives, and treat them with respect...so that nothing will hinder your prayers" (1 Peter 3:7, NIV).

The husband who does not respect his wife is like one who despises his helper.

To say the least, it is not wise to ignore aid and advice that is given in your best interest.

Finally, we note that wives and husbands alike are commanded to respect one another.

Red Sails in the Sunset

In summation, the best way to have a marriage that is full of beautiful red sails in the sunset is for the couple to learn when to set sail and when to drop anchor.

Four

The Ezer K'negdo

Why is my wife always against me? the rabbi asked himself.

His detailed study of the Hebrew words used to describe his "help meet" soon revealed the truth.

The rabbi found that, whereas woman was created to be a help to her husband, she was also created to be "against" her husband.

What is this *helper* created to be *against?*

Every wrong thing her mate might want to do!

Woman was created to be a "help meet."

The King James phrase, "help meet" is translated from the Hebrew words, *"ezer k'negdo."*

"YHVH Elohim said, 'It is not good that the man should be alone; I will make him an *help meet* for him'" (Genesis 2:18, KJV).

In Hebrew, "an help meet for..." reads, עֵזֶר כְּנֶגְדּוֹ It means a helper corresponding to him in kind, or a helper against.

Strong's Exhaustive Hebrew Concordance says the word "*ezer*" means *help, one who helps, succors (supports, aids, helps)*.

The word is used 22 times in the King James Bible and 21 times it is translated *help*.

Once, in Genesis 2:20, *ezer* is translated as "meet." There, the word is used consecutively ("*ezer, ezer*") and so is translated "help meet." [3]

This is so because among the animals, Adam could not find a "helper" that was "meet" for him, meaning *a true help* to him, so Abba created Eve.

The word "*neged*" means conspicuous, in front or in sight of, before your face or eyes, in your view or purpose, corresponding to, parallel to, straight forward, over, before the eyes of, opposite.

This word is used (in the KJV) a total of 167 times and is primarily translated as "before (82 times), as "over" (27 times), and as "against" (34 times).[4]

The word is rooted in *nagad*, which means, "properly to front, stand boldly opposite; to manifest; figuratively to announce (by word of mouth) specifically to expose, predict, explain, praise.[5]

When put together in the above Hebrew verse, the words are pronounced *"ezer k'negdo."*

- *"Ezer"* means help or helper.
- *"K"* means like, about, or as.
- *"Neged"* means opposite, facing, parallel to, or corresponding to.
- The *"O"* suffix indicates that it speaks of Adam.

Ezer K'negdo — "Helper corresponding to..."

(Thanks to Rimona Frank, Hebrew Editor, for this translation.)

---

3 *Strong's Concordance*, and *Brown, Driver, Briggs Hebrew Lexicon*, word # H5828. Hereafter these reference books will be referred to as *Strong's* and *BDB*.
4 *Strong's* # H5048.
5 *Strong's* # H5046.

Our Call As Women

Women can see shadows of their call to their husbands in the above word descriptions.

Among other things, we are to announce the truth, expose anything that might hinder our mate, and to predict, to the best of our ability, what we feel lies ahead. Additionally, we are to praise him.

Although husbands are in many ways the stronger of the two, they nonetheless need, and even thrive on, the true praises of their wives.

Therefore, to correspond to and enhance the purposes of men the world over, the Father created the female—as an *ezer*, a helper.

The Ezer in Scripture

The word *ezer* does not speak of an inferior status.

It is used 22 times, 5 of which refer to the woman created in the image of the Almighty, 3 times to military aid, and 14 times to the Almighty Himself!

Reading verses about an *ezer* can help paint a picture of what it means to be one. Even if the verse speaks of military aid, or of the Almighty, we can nonetheless imagine ways in which the principles involved might be applied to women.

- Moses said, "God...was my *ezer*, and delivered me from the sword of Pharaoh" (Exodus 18:4).
- Praying for Judah, Moses said: "O YHVH.... be his *ezer* against his foes" (Deuteronomy 33:7).
- "There is none like Elohim...Who rides the heavens to your *ezer*" (Deuteronomy 33:26).
- Blessed are you, O Israel...YHVH...is the shield of your *ezer*, and your glorious sword" (Deuteronomy 33:29).
- "We wait for YHVH; He is our *ezer* and our shield" (Psalm 33:20, NIV).

- YHVH will "send you *ezer* from the sanctuary, and will support, refresh and strengthen you from Zion" (Psalm 20:2, AMP).
- "Come quickly O God. You are my *ezer*, my deliverer; O Lord, do not delay" (Psalm 70:5, NIV).
- "Once You spoke in a vision to Your devoted one and said, I have endowed one who is mighty (a hero, giving him the power to *ezer*— to be a champion for Israel)" (Psalm 87:19, AMP).
- YHVH said, "I have bestowed strength [*ezer*], on a warrior; I have exalted a young man from among the people" (Psalm 89:19, NIV).
- "O Israel, trust and take refuge in YHVH! (Lean on, rely on and be confident in Him!) He is your *ezer* and shield" (Psalm 115:9, AMP).
- "And I shall scatter... his helpers [*ezer*] and all his troops" (Ezekiel 12:14).
- "Everyone will be put to shame because of a people useless to them, who bring neither *ezer* nor advantage, but only shame and disgrace" (Isaiah 30:5, NIV).
- "When they fall, they will receive a little *ezer*, many who are not sincere will join them" (Daniel 11:34).
- "You are destroyed, O Israel, because you are against Me, against your helper [*ezer*]" (Hosea 13:9).

Made in the Image of The Ezer of Ezers

Yahveh Elohim Himself is an *ezer*.

He is our righteous right arm of deliverance. And He created woman in His image—as an *ezer*.

An Ezer: A Scriptural Portrait

- An *ezer* is a deliverer, a help against foes—one who comes from the Heavenlies—like a shield and glorious sword.
- An *ezer* is useful, quick to respond, and brings refreshing help from the Holy Place.
- An *ezer* is like warring troops who bring advantage and not disgrace.
- An *ezer* is a trusted refuge, and a strong champion—a champion for Israel.

Words of Wisdom for Helpers and Husbands

Those who were created to be an *ezer* would do well to realize that:

- The help of an *ezer* can and will be measured
- You can be a little help or a lot of help.

We want to be women who are a lot of help.

We never want our words to our husbands to be words that tear him down. Like the woman of Proverbs 31, so the hearts of our husbands hearts must be able to trust in us (vs 31:11).

A word of wisdom for the husband:

- He who is against his *ezer* is destroyed.

The man who does not appreciate his wife as a God-given *ezer*, will find that both his life and his prayers are hindered:

"You husbands in the same way, live with your wives in an understanding way...and show her honor as a fellow heir of the grace of life, so that your prayers will not be hindered" (1 Peter 3:7).

Helpful Quotes:

"The term *ezer* (one who *helps*) does not at all imply inherent subordination. The term *helper* most frequently refers to God…and sometimes…to military protectors and allies…. If being *one who helps* inherently implies subordination, then in that case, God would be subordinate to humans!" (*Beyond the Curse* by A'ida B. Spencer, Thomas Nelson, Nashville, 1985, pp 25-27).

"*Ezer* in no way suggests a subordinate. On the contrary, it is used in the Old Testament mainly of God who *helps* and delivers His people" (*Equal Woman* by Myrtle Langley, Hansing, 1983, p 51).

"'*Ezer kenegdo* is translated: 'an *helpmeet* for him' (KJV): 'a *helper* fit for him' (RSV): and 'a *helpmate*' (JERUSB). *Ezer* is the noun for *help*. *Kenegdo* means according to what is in front of…a corresponding help…equal and adequate to himself. She completes Adam, working with him in carrying out the plan of God." (*Wycliffe Bible Encyclopedia,* Moody, Chicago, 1995, pp 779-780).

"R. David Freedman argues that the Hebrew word *ezer* etymologically derives from the merger of two Semitic roots, *zr*, 'to save, rescue' and *gzr* 'to be strong.' He says this passage has reference to the latter: woman is created, like the man, 'a power (or strength) superior to the animals'" (*Woman, A Power Equal to Man*, Biblical Archaeology Review Magazine, Jan-Feb. 1983, pp 56-58).

According to the famous rabbi, Rashi, the term *ezer k'negeo* can either mean a helper, as in front of him, or a helper against him (Rashi 2:18). He moreover "explains that if man is worthy, the woman will be a helper (*ezer*); if he proves unworthy, she shall be against him (*k'negdo*)" (*Jewish Wedding Guide*, Amy J. Kramer, www.everythingjewish.com).

Bringing Shame or Glory

The word *ezer* carries no implication of female sub-ordination, nor position of assistant as opposed to a shared partnership. It implies a submitted role as one who *chooses* to come alongside to help.

Our God similarly chooses this role when He comes alongside us to help us, for He comes to us as a Servant (Isaiah 49:3; Luke 22:24-27).

The forming of woman from man demonstrates the fundamental unity and equality of human beings. The word *k'negdo* (suitable) denotes correspondence to Adam's need, or lack. It indicates equality and adequacy, as in completion and not subordination.

While woman was created to be against any wrong ideas her mate might have, she also is to be against any wrong that might possibly come against him. By choosing to serve in this way, she is a true help.

In the male and female we see traits in each that the other lacks, thus the need for one another as complements who help to fulfill the other. Because of the way we are made, man has a deep need for woman. And woman has an amazing God-given ability, even a power, to bring shame, or respect and glory, to her husband (1 Corinthians 11:7-12).

We must realize that just as husbands have a certain power over their wives, so the wife has a certain power over her husband.

Thus a wife would do well to determine in her heart that she will use her position with her mate to bring glory to him.

The Book of Proverbs lists many of the attributes, giftings, and freedoms the Almighty gave to woman.

These verses are recited the world over on Shabbat evenings, when women recite Psalm 1 over their husbands, and husbands recite Proverbs 31 over their wives. Both are meant as blessings.

Proverbs 31:10-31 —

An excellent wife, who can find? Her worth is far above jewels. The heart of her husband trusts in her, and he will have no lack of gain. She does him good and not evil all the days of her life. She looks for wool and flax and works with her hands in delight. She is like merchant ships; she brings her food from afar. She rises also while it is still night and gives food to her household and portions to her maidens. She considers a field and buys it; from her earnings she plants a vineyard. She girds herself with strength and makes her arms strong. She senses that her gain is good; her lamp does not go out at night. She stretches out her hands to the distaff, and her hands grasp the spindle. She extends her hand to the poor, and she stretches out her hands to the needy. She is not afraid of the snow for her household, for all her household are clothed with scarlet. She makes coverings for herself; her clothing is fine linen and purple. Her husband is known in the gates, when he sits among the elders of the land. She makes linen garments and sells them, and supplies belts to the tradesmen. Strength and digni-ty are her clothing, and she smiles at the future. She opens her mouth in wisdom, and the teaching of kindness is on her tongue. She looks well to the ways of her household, and does not eat the bread of idle-ness. Her children rise up and bless her; her husband also, and he praises her, saying: "Many daughters have done nobly, but you excel them all." Charm is deceitful and beauty is vain, but a woman who fears YHVH, she shall be praised. Give her the product of her hands, and let her works praise her in the gates.

*May all the women of Israel be so blessed
as to walk in the footsteps of this noble woman.*

Five

Mama's Torah

ear, my son, your father's instruction, and do not forsake the teaching of your mother. Indeed, they are a graceful wreath to your head and ornaments about your neck." And, "My son, observe the commandment of your father, and do not forsake the teaching of your mother, bind them continually on your heart; tie them around your neck. When you walk about, they will guide you; when you sleep, they will watch over you; and when you awake, they will talk to you" (Proverbs 1:8-9, 6:20-22).

Even as we must understand what the Father had in mind when He created woman as an *ezer k'negdo*, so we must envision the role He originally intended for women to play in establishing His eternal truths among mankind. For if we do not build according to His divine plan, we labor in vain. We build but sand castles destined to be washed away with the tides of time.

In the above verses about the "teachings" of our mothers we see a principle that reveals much about how truth is to be conveyed to our Father's children. However, to more fully apprehend the truths hidden in these verses we must first examine a few of the Hebrew words being used.

We begin with the Hebrew word for "hear" in Proverbs 1:8. It is a root word, *shama*, which means to listen to with attention, to yield to, and to obey.[6] This word is used because we need to yield our will to this instruction. It is important to our well being.

Father's Instruction

The word being translated father's "instruction" is the Hebrew word, מוּסָר musar, which means, discipline, chastening, correction.[7]

Mother's Torah/Teaching

The word translated your mother's "teaching" is actually the Hebrew word תֹּורָה / תֹּרָה — torah. It is the same word used to speak of the "Torah," or Law, that was given to Moses.

Twice in Scripture we read of our "mother's torah."

"Hear, my son, your father's instruction and do not forsake your mother's *torah*; indeed, they are a graceful wreath to your head and ornaments about your neck" (Proverbs 1:8-9). And, "My son, observe the commandment of your father and do not forsake the *torah* of your mother. Bind them continually on your heart; tie them around your neck. When you walk about, they will guide you; when you sleep, they will watch over you; and when you awake, they will talk to you" (Proverbs 6:20-22).

---

6 *Strong's* and *BDB* word # H8085.
7 *Strong's* and *BDB* word # H4148.

Torah means law, direction, instruction (human or divine).[8]

Concerning this most important word, we must realize that while Scripture does speak of our "mother's torah," there is no mention in the Word of an earthly "father's torah."

Instead, we see mention of the Torah of YHVH, which He *gave* to our forefathers (2 Kings 17:13).

Scripture makes no specific mention of a "father's torah," but, we do read of mother's torah.

Why?

The Heart of the Home

Mothers establish the *heart* of the home, which is why YHVH is against the idea of the children of Israel having "foreign wives" (Ezra 10:10).

Foreign wives establish foreign ways in the hearts and homes of His children, and Abba does not want that for us.

Children are trained early in life, thus they first need "godly mothers."

That is how we develop *natural*, or *cultivated*, vines (Romans 11), meaning children nurtured and trained in the ways of the Holy One.[9]

The Holy One uses the mothers of Israel to help Him write the foundational principles of His Instructions on the hearts of the children of Israel— He uses mothers to impart the *spirit* of His Torah.

---

8 *Strong's* and *BDB* word # H8451.
9 See *Who Is Israel? Past, Present, and Future* by Batya Ruth Wootten, Chap. 20, *Paul's Olive Tree*, Key of David Publishing, St Cloud, FL, 2003.

Once babies are weaned from their mother's milk, they are turned over to their fathers, who then begin a different type of training.

The father teaches the child about the commandments of the Holy One. Traditionally, he prepares his son to become "Bar Mitzvah," which means to become a "Son of the Commandments."

Daughters are in turn trained for a "Bat Mitzvah," which means "Daughter of the Commandments."

This event marks a time when the child becomes accountable for his actions: "When I was a child, I used to speak like a child, think like a child, reason like a child; when I became a man, I did away with childish things" (1 Corinthians 13:11).

A Bar Mitzvah normally takes place in the life of a Jewish child when they begin their thirteenth year.

Our Messiah may have participated in this special "rite of passage." We know that His family regularly went up to Jerusalem to honor the feasts. And assuming Messiah Yeshua was born on the first day of Tabernacles, and circumcised its "eighth day," then at the time of His thirteenth birthday His family would have been in Jerusalem. There, they could readily gather their family members for the occasion (Luke 2:42-47; 1:59; Leviticus 25:35-36).[10]

Our Scriptural Pattern for Development

Returning to the instructions found in our above "Mama's Torah" verses, we see a very enlightening Biblical principle:

A.   First mama nurtures the children.
B.   Then they are ready to hear papa's principles.

---

10 Also see Lev 12:3, and *Israel's Feasts and their Fullness* by Batya Ruth Wootten, chapters, "He Came To Tabernacle Among Us," and, "The Roots of Christmas," Key of David, Saint Cloud, FL. 2002.

Different Types of Training

Mothers and fathers give children different types of training. The female expression of mankind is often said to be spirit-led, whereas the male expression tends to be more analytical.

A good combination of these types of instruction will prove to be as graceful wreaths to our heads and ornaments about our necks. We are to bind this balanced type of training on our hearts. As we walk about it will guide us; when we sleep, it will watch over us, and when we awake, it will talk to us.

The intuitive truths taught to us by our mothers will especially be with us in prayer, will complain to us when we are disobedient, and will even declare and confirm truth to us—for hers tend to be "spirit words" that speak to our inner man.

We Begin With Nurturing Truth

Our first encounter with the truths of Torah should be as easy to digest, and as delightful to us as mother's milk. The teachings should first be warm, soothing, nurturing. Like mother's milk, this will build up our immune systems and make our bodies strong.

Although "motherly truths" are basic, they nonetheless must be part of our foundation. The principles that mother teaches are part of our essence and vital to our well being. For, if we do not first learn to nurse at the breast of mercy, to suckle at the bosom of kindness, we will not grow properly, nor be truly empowered to do the Father's will.

> *We must learn to nurse at the breast of mercy, to suckle at the bosom of kindness...*

We need the immunity from evil that mother's milk supplies. Being properly rooted in the basics will help us to ward off evil, even the "disease" of HaSatan, the Accuser.

The problem is that few of us have been properly nurtured, and we must have this essential element if we are to become true sons and daughters of the commandments. We need to personally know the taste of mother's milk, that we might in turn be able to teach truth in a way that nurtures the hearer.

Mama's Torah—Papa's Principles

Mother's torah-milk is much like the elementary, yet foundational, principles of our faith: Repentance from dead works, faith toward God, instruction about *baptisms/mikvehs*, laying on of hands, resurrection of the dead, eternal judgment. It also is like the gentle fruits of the Spirit: Love, joy, peace, patience, kindness, goodness, faithfulness, gentleness, self-control (Hebrews 6:1-3; Galatians 5:23).

In Micah 6:8 we read, "He has told you, O man, what is good; and what does YHVH require of you but to do justice, to love kindness, and to walk humbly with your God?"

Justice, kindness, and humility are innate qualities that are first learned from our mothers. They are not to be initially taught and then forgotten, but are instead foundational to our adult walk.

The father's instructions have to do with the "jot and tittle of Torah." He deals with the "instruction and correction" related to the finer points of the Law. He deals with the "meat" of faith, which has to do with the practical application of actually *doing* the will of our Father in Heaven. For, as Messiah Yeshua explained, "My *meat* is to do the will of him that sent me, and to finish his work" (John 4:34, KJV).

Earthly father's are called to represent the Heavenly Father's love to the family. The man is the "officer in charge" if you will, and needs to see that all is well with those whom he is chosen to oversee.

Getting It By The Spirit

Although Scripture does not specifically define "the torah of thy mother," nonetheless, our heavenly Father apparently placed great importance on its role in our lives. Why so?

Again, woman is intuitive and tends to be "spirit-led." Thus, we see that the Father intended that His Word should first be understood "by the spirit."

Mothers deal with heart attitudes and focus on their child's *character*. They watch over their child's relationships with their siblings, ever giving instructions like:

"You watch out for each other now!"

"You all kiss and make up."

"You children play nice together."

Such commands are abstract in that they do not tell you exactly how to "play nice." However, they are usually quickly understood by children, because they are matters of the heart, and children listen more with the heart than they do with the intellect, which is why we need to become like little children if we want to see the kingdom of Heaven (Matthew 18:3).

When we were children, we quickly understood motherly instructions like:

"You wipe that look off your face right now!"

Although commands like this are not very precise, when spoken sharply by a mother, most children do not need a lot of teaching, or "jot and tittle" of the law, to know that it is time to shape up or else you are in big trouble!

From Mother to Father

We see an example of a mother turning a child over to the father for correction in a typical scenario that most of us have probably lived through.

The mother says to the child, *"If you don't stop this and behave, I am going to tell your father when he comes home!"*

Mama deals with heart motives.

Papa corrects wrong actions in the walk.

The Sadness of It All

Many are now lamenting the fact that the people have "thrown God out of the schools."

Crime is up and morality is down.

It is as many bemoan. "What can you expect?" they ask. "We told the Almighty that we did not want Him in the schools, and being a gentleman, He left. Now our children don't know Him as they should."

Similarly, it is sad beyond words that man has essentially silenced the vessel through whom the Father would have His Torah instructions begin.

In this case, silence is not golden.

It is instead darkness.

Quieting the women of the Judeo-Christian world has helped to create the unbalanced religious realm in which we now must live.

To see the world as the Father planned it, women must be allowed to speak without feeling recrimination because they are women.

Only then will the Spirit be free to move among us.

Women are told not to speak, and wanting to be obedient, many are reluctant to voice their opinions in congregational settings. Quieting women in this way results in gentleness not being revered as it should be. Silencing the females tends to reap the same sad results as does forbidding mention of our God in our public schools. Meanness goes up and kindness goes down when we stifle our God and our women.

Legalism and lawlessness are likewise on the increase among us. And women especially can help alleviate the situation. However, to accomplish this goal, we must cease to be afraid to allow women to share what the Almighty has shown them.

Weep and wail O people of Israel.
Moan for the sadness of it all.
Beseech the Father. Ask Him to take away the blinders that we might see. Ask Him to please allow us to nurse at the breast of mercy, to feed at the bosom of lovingkindness.

Six

The Women of
the Old Covenant

*T*he women of the *Tenach* (the Old Covenant) set a certain standard for all the women who have come after them.

As Believers in the Messiah of Israel, we build on the foundation of Torah, on the Prophets and the Writings. To this foundation we add our New Covenant understandings.

Each of these—Torah, Prophets, the Writings, and the New Covenant, or *Brit HaDoshah*—should be building on, enhancing, *and not contradicting*, the other. For our God is the same yesterday, today, and forever. He does not lie, and He does not change (Hebrews 13:8; Malachi 3:6).

With this idea in mind, we will continue to build on our understanding of the call of women by briefly examining their role in Scripture.

To begin, we note that Rav Hollisa Alewine, in a

paper entitled, *Women in Ministry,* points out that we must build on that which is taught in the *Tenach,* and that Messiah Yeshua Himself instructed His disciples "beginning with the Torah, the Prophets, and the Psalms." [11]

We want to do the same. Moreover, we realize that the *Brit Hadoshah* should never be interpreted in a way that violates the foundations established in the *Tenach.* And in that Holy Book we see that...

- Miriam was a co-leader with Moses and Aaron: Micah 6:4, "...I sent Moses to lead you, also Aaron and Miriam."
  Miraim was a prophetess, a worship leader, and a leader of women.
- Women apparently were singers in the Temple (Ezra 2:64).
- Huldah was an advisor to King Josiah and to the High Priest Hilkiah (2 Kings 22:11-20).
  Huldah had a powerful prophetic anointing and King Josiah sought her advice. He even sent six men to receive God's word from her, which resulted in a national revival.[12]
- Deborah, or D'vorah, was both a judge and a military leader (Judges 4:4-5:31).
  Judges 5:7 tells us, "The rulers ceased in Israel, until thou didst arise, Deborah..."
  In Judges 5:13 we read that D'vorah said, "YHVH made me have dominion over the mighty."
  This woman urged military leader Barak to arise and take command of the troops, but he refused to do so unless D'vorah would continue as his co-leader.

---

11 *Women in Ministry,* Olive Branch Reading File, www.israelnet.tv.
12 See "A Study in Paul's View" by Lenore Lindsey Mullican; http://members.cox.net/8thday/women.html

- Queen Esther, or Hadassah, was a Lawgiver. To this day the Jewish community annually honors her commands to fast and pray. Esther was a deliverer who proclaimed Jewish fast and feast days. These days are now known as *Purim*.
Esther 9:29 tells us, "So Queen Esther wrote with full authority to confirm...Purim."

Thus the following positions should potentially be open to women:

- Co-leader (with Moses no less!)
- Prophetess
- Worship Leader
- Leader of Women
- Temple Singer
- Advisor to Kings and High Priests
- Judge
- Military Leader
- Queen
- Lawgiver
- Maker of Proclamations

Working With Male Leadership

Now before we go off running and leaping and claiming that we women can do *anything*, let us first note an important point about each of these women: Each one appears to have been working in concert with a family member or in harmony with some form of male headship.

Miriam worked with Moses. The singers worked with the priests. Huldah worked with King Josiah. Deborah worked with her husband, and with Barak. And Esther worked with her relative, Mordechai.

On the other hand, we note that even though each of these women appear to have been working in harmony with male leadership, they nonetheless acted in leadership capacities themselves.

For example, Deborah did not go to her husband, nor to Barak, to inquire about the word of the Lord. No. The Father gave His word directly to her. Yet, she worked in concert with the men the Father had placed in her life.

We who follow in the footsteps of these women should have similar doors open to us in our day.

To refuse any of these positions to women is to take from them positions the Almighty has already granted that they might walk in.

With this understanding in place we now move toward an examination of the women listed in the "New and Better Covenant."

Seven

The Women of the New Covenant

*I*n the *Brit Hadoshah*, which is a "new and better" Covenant than the Old/First Covenant (Hebrews 12:24), we see the following:

- Phoebe is called a deacon, or "*diakonos*," for which there is no feminine appellation. She was a co-laborer in apostleship (Romans 16:1-2). This word was translated *deacon* in the KJV when it dealt with men, but was translated *succoror* in Phoebe's case, which may show a deliberate bias against females.

- Junia is referred to as an apostle (Romans 16:7). Some manuscripts were later deliberately changed to read *Junias*, which is a man's name.[13]

---

13 *A Study in Paul's View* by Lenore Mullican: http://members.cox.net /8thday/women.html.

- Euodias and Syntyche are called co-workers of the apostle Paul (Philippians 4:2-3).
- Priscilla and Aquila were called apostles and teachers. They established congregations and discipled many. They were Paul's missionary companions, and Priscilla (Prisca) took part in instructing the learned Apollos (Acts 18:26).
- The women at Corinth were praying and prophesying, which is what Peter said Joel had said would happen (Acts 2:17-18; Joel 2:28; 1 Corinthians 11:5-6). Plus Philip had four daughters that prophesied (Acts 21:9).
- A nucleus of women developed the church at Phillipi (Acts 16:12-15,40).
- Women gave direction to various churches that met in their homes (Acts 12:12; Colossians 4:15; 1 Corinthians 1:11; 16:19; Romans 16:2-5; Philemon 2; 2 John 1:1).
- Anna ministered with fasting and prayer daily in the Temple. She was the first evangelist for Yeshua, preceding even Yochanan/John the Baptist (Luke 2:36).
- "Mary was listening to the Lord, sitting at His feet" (Luke 10:39). To sit at the feet of a great rabbi was to sit in a place of honor. We see this in that the learned Paul was said to be "educated at the feet of Gamaliel" (Acts 22:3).
- The first person ever to declare the message that "He is risen!" was Mary Magdalene. She did this based on Messiah Yeshua's specific instructions to her, and she proclaimed that most important message to none other than the apostles (John 20:17).
- In Joppa there was a disciple named Tabitha (or Dorcas) who was abounding with deeds of kindness and charity (Acts 9:36).

Based on this list of notable women of the New Covenant, we see that women in our day should potentially have open to them positions such as:

- Deacon
- Apostle
- Co-worker of Apostles
- Missionary
- Instructor of the Learned
- Prayer Warrior and Intercessor
- Prophetess
- Church/Congregational Planter/Director
- Preacher of the Good News
- Evangelist
- Student of Rabbis (why learn if you can't teach?)
- Disciple
- Worker of Charity

Our believing communities should be aligned with the Biblical patterns of the Scripture. And while it clearly depicts a pattern of male leadership, it also clearly shows female participation.

Archaeological finds, dating as far back as the First Century BC, similarly demonstrate that women held leadership positions in the synagogues of ancient Israel. There is evidence written in stone of women functioning as "Head of the Synagogue," "Mother of the Synagogue," and "Elder." [14]

We must continue in the Biblical pattern that has been set for us. The women of today must be allowed to freely walk in the same positions of faith their

---

14 See *A Study in Paul's View* by Lenore Lindsey Mullican, professor, Oral Roberts University: www.members.cox.net/8thday/women.html; *The Role of Women in First-Century Judaism and the Church* by Dr. Roy Blizzard, Yavo Digest, 1987: http://webbpage.topcities.com/Yavo/1_4_Bliz_WomensRole.html; and, Bernadette J. Brooten, *Women Leaders in the Ancient Synagogue*. Atlanta: Scholar's Press, 1982.

.

predecessors once walked in. They must be encouraged to walk in the offices long ago granted to them, as described in Old Covenant and New. To do anything less is to be unfaithful to the Word—Genesis to Revelation. It is to go against the Father's plan of redemption for all His children.

We must understand that we serve a God who will allow His children to keep going around the mountain until they finally get it right. So let us receive the truth about women and thereby release half of our army, that we might be empowered to move on, into the Promised Land.

Eight

Women and the World of Paul

ncient Israel. The name calls to mind an ideal of Biblical purity for some. However, those who know the truth of history know that many of the ages past were not times wherein women were properly honored.

In ancient Israel, many men would not even speak to their wives in public,[15] which may explain why the disciples were "amazed" to see Messiah Yeshua speaking openly to the Samaritan woman at the well (John 4:27).

Messiah Yeshua openly spoke to women because He was a liberator of women. He even had a woman declare the greatest message of all time—to the most important men in the church/*ekklesia*/congregation.

---

15 See *What Paul Really Said About Women*, John Temple Bristow "Where the Idea Began," pp 18-19. Harper Collins, San Francisco. 1991.

At the behest of the Master Himself, Mary Magdalene preached resurrection truth to the disciples, telling them that their *Moshiach*, their Anointed One, had risen from the dead.

Yeshua's own mother was a true stalwart of the faith. Accepting the offer to bear a child before she came to be with her husband could have cost her very life. She could have been stoned to death for saying "Behold, the bond-slave of the Lord; may it be done to me according to your word" (Luke 1:38).

Surely Messiah Yeshua was raised by a bold woman. Little wonder that He was not afraid to allow women to speak the truth. Perhaps this is one reason why so many of them followed Him (Matthew 27:55).

But such was not the case with many of the men at that time...

Women and Ancient Greece

To grasp the truths that Paul wrote about in his various Letters, we first need to understand the degradations women were being subjected to during his lifetime. We need to envision the social scene in order to see what Paul's arguments were actually about, because most of the difficult passages he wrote have to do with cultural problems.

John Temple Bristow paints a picture of the cultures and times of Paul in his book, *What Paul Really Said About Women.*[16]

Bristow details the situation in ancient Greece and Palestine (as it was then known), showing that philosophers like Socrates, Plato, Aristotle, and others, declared many profane things about women.

Licentiousness was rampant, and they blamed the problem on women,

---

16 Harper Collins, San Francisco. 1991. Note: This book and others like it are listed in the Recommended Reading section of this book.

Women were used, abused, and hidden away. A silent woman was said to be a good woman.

Women also were thought to be lesser beings. Socrates argued that being born a woman was a punishment, since woman supposedly was *not* taken from man, as Scripture clearly declares. Instead, these men and their followers taught that a woman was "halfway between a man and an animal." [17]

Man, on the other hand, was thought to be greater because he was created before woman. However, Bristow argues that if this idea were followed through to its logical conclusion, then cows must be superior to man, because they were created prior to man, and fish were created before cows, and so on (page 17).

Women and Ancient Ephesus

Women suffered a different fate in immoral Ephesus.

In their book, *I Suffer Not a Woman*, Richard and Catherine Kroger paint a picture that shows cult prostitution ruling the day. [18]

They explain that it was generally believed that Eve brought sexual enlightenment to man. Cult prostitutes were thought to be effecting a contact with the gods, bringing about a "sacred marriage" between the "worshiper" and their god. Through these sexual unions, the priestesses supposedly brought salvation to men. Thus, these women were viewed as "mediators," and in this way they spiritually "ruled over" the men they served.

The cult priestesses in essence ruled the temples, because the cults were sexually oriented and could not survive without the favors of the female.

On one hand, women were treated as outcasts, but on the other, their favors were sought out. Ironically,

---

17 Bristow p 4.
18 1992, Baker Book House, Grand Rapids, MI.

those said to be less than human also were thought to be more spiritual than their male counterpart.

Paul's letters addressed these and other problems that were impacting the Believers of the Early Church. However, the words of this apostle have often been misunderstood.

Paul: Liberator of Women

Bristow says of the way Paul's writings are presently translated into English:

"If I took our English translation of his words and translated them back into Greek, my words should be similar to Paul's original words. But when I tried doing this, such was not the case, not at all! In reality, the words that Paul chose to use imply different ideas from those conveyed by the English words we use to translate his writings. In fact, our English words imply ideas that Paul deliberately avoided!" [19]

The idea that women were inferior infiltrated much of the ancient world, and Paul warred against it.

How sad that someone who wanted to help the situation should have his words mistranslated and used against the very ones he wanted to help.

The Most Misunderstood Man in History

Shaul of Tarsus may well be the most misunderstood man in all of history. Peter even said of him: "Our beloved brother Paul, according to the wisdom given him, wrote to you, as also in all his letters, speaking in them of these things, in which are some things hard to understand, which the untaught and unstable distort, as they do also the rest of the Scriptures, to their own destruction" (2 Peter 3:16).

---

19 *Ibid.* Preface, p xi.

Such was the case in the time of the apostles, and such is the case in our day. Many have misrepresented and misunderstood Paul's teachings, both about the Law, and about women.[20]

Speak or Chatter?

We are told that Paul forbade women to "speak" in churches. However, Richard and Catherine Kroeger address this issue in their book, *I Suffer Not A Woman*.[21] They postulate that the word being translated *speak* can legitimately be translated as *chatter*. Thus, we Paul telling the women to stop their endless *chatter* during the congregational meetings.

Paul was not excluding the women. He wanted them to join in, but did not want them chattering about their babies and recipes as though they were not called to learn the principles of Torah. So he told them to "subject themselves" to the studies, to sit quietly and learn, just as the Torah teaches them to do (1 Corinthians 14:34).

Forbidden to Speak?

In 1 Corinthians 14:34-35, we read:

"Women are to keep silent in the churches; for they are not permitted to speak/chatter, but are to subject themselves, just as the Law also says. If they desire to learn anything, let them ask their own husbands at home; for it is improper for a woman to speak/chatter in church."

Three chapters earlier, Paul affirmed that women could "pray and prophesy" (verses 11:5-6), which proves that women *were* "speaking" in the meetings.

---

20 See *Who is Israel? Past, Present, and Future*, 2003, chapters 25-28; also *Israel's Feasts and their Fullness* 2002, Addendum B: "Paul and the Feasts" by Batya Wootten. Key of David Publishing, Saint Cloud, FL,
21 1992, Baker Book House, Grand Rapids, MI.

If we take his statement to mean that a woman literally cannot "speak" in church, then she cannot even yell *"Fire!"* in an emergency. That is foolishness.

Paul probably told the women of Corinth to "keep silence" because some of them were former worshipers of Dionysus—the god of wine and madness. His female followers were known as, *maenads*, or *mad ones*, because their loud, frenzied shouting at ceremonial events often resulted in riots.[22]

The Greek verb translated "remain silent" in essence means to keep your peace, to control yourself, to refrain from speaking out of respect, just as we do not talk during prayer or a performance.[23]

Four verses earlier, this word is translated exactly this way in the King James: "If any thing be revealed to another that sitteth by, let the first *hold his peace*" (1 Corinthians 14:30, KJV).

What's A Touchdown?

We can liken this exchange to a group of people who are watching a football game at home, and some of the wives know nothing about football.

Then, just as the ball is flying through the air, and everyone is excitedly yelling, "It's gonna be a touchdown," one unknowing woman calls out to her husband, who is sitting across the room...

"Honey, what's a touchdown?"

There is a time and a place for questions, and they ought not be asked when it will disrupt everything for the many.

---

22 Also see, *The Apostle Paul and the Greco-Roman Cults of Women* by C. Kroeger, Journal of the Evangelical Theological Society, March, 1987, p. 25: www.cbeinternational.org. And, "The Corinthian female dominated religious...practice. From the mother goddess Artemis to the women serving...as temple prostitutes and speaking messages from the gods, the male of Corinth was...dependent upon the female." *A Study in Paul's View* by Lenore L. Mullican, Oral Roberts Univ: www.members.cox.net.
23 *Strong's* word # G4601.

Decorum In Worship

Paul was addressing the issue of *order* in this letter. He was explaining when to speak and when to defer to others in a meeting (verse 14:40).

These women were not addressing the assembly as leaders, but were *chattering* during the service, thus disturbing others. So Paul told them to be quiet, and to maintain congregational order. He was establishing order, not forever quieting women.

As for submission, the women, like the men, were being called to submit to the general rules of order and decorum. Decorum in worship is a primary theme here. The topic is order in the congregation. It is not about the intrinsic value of women, nor their qualifications for leadership. [24]

Messianic Rules Concerning Paul

The Messianic world has essentially concluded that if we take Paul's writings out of context, as it is believed that many in the institutional Church have done, we are ultimately led to abolish:

- The Torah and the Prophets
- The Scripturally Kosher diet
- Sabbath and New Moons
- The Feasts of Israel
- Allowing Physical Circumcision as a Covenant Sign

Most Messianic Believers refuse to do this.

However, if this is our standard, then we likewise should not allow mistaken teachings to hinder women who want to walk in their God-given roles.

---

24 See *Strong's* word # G2980; www.kencollins.com/question-32.htm; http://lists.ibiblio.org/pipermail/b-greek/1998-August/001203.html; www.wag.org.nz/Studies/Series/Women/Silent.htm; www.christianed ucational.org/pdf/handouts/0502_Role_of_Women.pdf

If we want to be a people who grasp the truth of what Paul was actually saying to the people about the problems of their time, then we must apply the same standard of "examining statements in context" to his teachings about women.

Paul used women as ministers and did *not* teach against them. He wanted them to be all that the Almighty had created them to be.

Paul was a champion of women's restoration.

We must seek to be the same.

Nine

Difficult Texts and Teachings

*E*ve ate of the forbidden fruit and it was thereafter decreed of all of her daughters, "Your desire shall be toward your husband, and he shall rule over you" (Genesis 3:16).

Like the "by the sweat of your brow" curse pronounced over her husband, so "ruling over the woman" is part of woman's curse for disobedience.

This ruling could not have been part of the original plan for our lives since it was decreed as part of our punishment. This is instead a product of sin, and thus should not be commended as though it were an ideal, for those who follow the Messiah are no longer under a curse (Galatians 3:10).

Nonetheless, some unenlightened men of the Old World thought women were little more than chattel —fleshy goods to be ruled over by man. Women everywhere have suffered from their mistaken ideas.

Since our God warned man in Deuteronomy 5:21 that he was "not to covet his neighbor's goods," and since wives were listed in this prohibition, along with servants, fields, and houses, some rabbis reasoned that women were "possessions."

John Bristow argues against this error. He notes that the fifth commandment tells us to "Honor your father *and your mother*." He points out that *things* cannot receive honor, but only *persons*, and thus this commandment gives equal value to a wife and mother as to a husband and father (see pages 18-22).

1 Corinthians 14:34-35 —

"Let the women *keep silence* in the churches...for they are not permitted to *speak*, but let them subject themselves, just as the Law also says. If they desire to learn anything, let them ask their own husbands at home" (1 Corinthians 14:34-35).

Again, these verses addressed disruptive chatter. Since the women of Corinth tended to equate "spirituality" with being "rowdy," and since they were not normally well versed in the Scriptures, Paul told them to ask their many questions of their more educated husbands at home.[25]

1 Timothy 2:12-14 —

"But I do not allow a woman to teach or exercise authority over a man, but to remain quiet. For it was Adam who was first created, and then Eve. And it was not Adam who was deceived, but the woman being deceived, fell into transgression. But women will be preserved through the bearing of children if they continue in faith and love and sanctity with self-restraint" (1 Timothy 2:12-15).

---

25 *The Apostle Paul and the Greco-Roman Cults of Women* by Catherine Kroeger, www.cbeinternational.org/shopsite_sc/store/html/page22.html

In his letters to the Corinthians and Ephesians (Timothy was in Ephesus when Paul wrote to him), Paul often had to address various heresies.

We see him refuting the idea that cult prostitutes are "mediators," as well as countering the idea that they are "more spiritual" than the men. Paul tells them that they do not spiritually "rule over" men.[26]

In addition, Paul affirms the men, declaring that there is but "one *mediator* between God and men, the man Christ Jesus" (1 Timothy 2:5). He is telling them that women are not the "only spiritual ones," as the cultists claim. He is encouraging them to believe in their own spiritual potential, and thus to begin to "pray, lifting up holy hands" (1 Timothy 2:8).

Can Women Teach?

Richard and Catherine Kroger address the issue of women teaching. They write:

"[T]he prohibition against teaching....comes in a letter which begins with an instruction that Timothy should prevent certain ones from teaching false doctrine (1:3-4). Titus is left behind (Titus 1:5) to appoint elders who will stop the mouth of the heretics (verse 11). [Does]...this prohibition refer to all Christian women, or simply to women heretics, to all Christian teachings or to wrong teaching[?].

"*Didaskein*...nearly always connotes the notion of 'teaching sound doctrine' or 'teaching error' in the Pastoral Epistles. Here it appears to...[connote] 'teach heresy.' In II Timothy 1:5...[and] 4:19....The author appears to be positive about the teaching of Christian women when it represents the truth. The problem lay with women who tried to assume the role of *mediator*.

"*Authentein*, the verb usually translated 'to rule over' or 'to dominate'...occurs only once in the entire Bible.

---

26 *I Suffer Not A Woman*, chapters 7 & 8.

However, its usual meaning...was to be responsible for a misdeed, usually murder. Thus we might translate 'I forbid a woman to teach or to murder a man.'...[The] priestesses of Artemis were sometimes required to consign men to their death (Read Euripides *Iphigenia at Tauris*...). ...Greek myths tell of a number of religiously-inspired murders of men by women. The last recorded human sacrifice made to Artemis occurred in the second century AD. Usually the slaughter was merely pantomime. ...[O]ne Christian cult, which revered Eve and was heavily dominated by women clergy, was accused of human sacrifice by other Christians.

"*Authentein* sometimes had a sexual connotation, and it may here refer to promiscuous rites by which women professed to teach men religious truths. We ...[see] this trait in Gnosticism, and it appears to have been an integral part of the pagan religion of Ephesus. Perhaps we should translate, 'I forbid a woman to instruct or initiate a man into fertility rites.'

"....Jewish tradition taught that it was Eve's seduction which brought death to humanity. In the New Testament, we also find the concept of seduction bringing death (Rom. 7:11).

"Another translation is also possible...'I forbid a woman to teach that she is superior to a man.'

"....Lastly, we are faced with the problem of 'salvation by childbearing' in I Tim. 2:15.

"Some Gnostics taught that women would be saved by becoming males and that Jesus had come to do away with the works of women, specifically childbearing. Thus verse 15 may be...declaring that women are saved as women and preserved in their childbearing function. They, like men, are saved by faith and free to retain their sexual identity and to serve as God may lead them." [27]

---

27 *Women Elders: Called by God?* by Richard and Catherine Kroeger: www.firstpresby.org/womenelders. Cindy Jacobs also affirms this view, translating the verse, "...or to proclaim herself the originator of man." *Women of Destiny*, Ventura, CA: Regal Books, 1998, p 241.

Jezebel...

Of all the claims that are used against women, few cut more deeply than does being called a "Jezebel." Women who seek to walk in right order can be stopped cold with this defaming title.

However, the shadow must fit the type, and if we examine Jezebel's actions, we find that crimes similar to hers are often committed by men.

Messiah Yeshua warned, "I have this against you, that you tolerate the woman Jezebel, who calls herself a prophetess, and she teaches and leads My bond-servants astray so that they commit acts of immorality and eat things sacrificed to idols. I gave her time to repent, and she does not want to repent of her immorality. Behold, I will throw her on a bed of sickness, and those who commit adultery with her into great tribulation, unless they repent of her deeds" (Revelation 2:20-22).

Seductive Queen Jezebel was the wife of Ahab, who was a king of the Northern Kingdom. Jezebel hindered and killed Israel's prophets, and she threatened Elijah. When Ahab coveted the field of Naboth the Jezreelite, but Naboth refused to sell his God-given inheritance, Jezebel swore that she would get the field for Ahab.[28]

To accomplish this takeover, she wrote lying letters to the elders in Ahab's name. The elders in turn conspired with her to give false testimony about Naboth's faith, and so to have him stoned to death.[29]

Painted Jezebel was thus guilty of harlotry and witchcraft. Her fate was to be eaten by the dogs, to be as dung on the fields of Jezreel (2 Kings 9:22-37).

---

28 Naboth means fruits, and Jezreel speaks of returning Ephraim (Hosea 1-2). Thus we see a type of the fruitful ones of returning Jezreel especially being attacked by the spirit of Jezebel. (See Hosea 1-2).
29 1 Kings 18:4,13; 19:1-3; 21:8-19.

Thus we see that Jezebel:

- Calls herself a prophetess
- Is seductive
- Teaches and leads bond-servants astray
- Encourages acts of immorality
- Eat things dedicated to idols
- Is not repentant
- Hinders Israel's prophets
- Threatens those anointed of the Lord
- Is covetous of the God-given property of others
- Works to take over the field of others
- Writes lying letters to the elders
- Encourages false testimony
- Practices harlotry and witchcraft

Jezebel wanted the field (ministry) of another, and would stop at nothing to get it.

When in the presence of anyone, man or woman, who exhibits these seductive, controlling, slanderous, and murderous traits, run for your spiritual life.

If you are in any way guilty of any of these sins, repent now and beg the Father for mercy.

1 Peter 3:3-5—

"Your adornment must not be merely external— braiding the hair, and wearing gold jewelry, or putting on dresses; but let it be the hidden person of the heart, with the imperishable quality of a gentle and quiet spirit, which is precious in the sight of God. For in this way in former times the holy women also, who hoped in God, used to adorn themselves, being submissive to their own husbands; just as Sarah obeyed Abraham, calling him lord, and you have become her children if you do what is right without being frightened by any fear."

Based on these verses, some churches mandate

bylaws that forbid women to wear any jewelry. However, we are destined to be Messiah's bride, and in Scripture, concerning the bride, we read: "He has clothed me with garments of salvation, He has wrapped me with a robe of righteousness...*as a bride adorns herself with her jewels*" (Isaiah 61:10).

Forgetting her special attire is compared to forgetting about our Lord: "Can a virgin forget her ornaments, or a bride her attire? Yet My people have forgotten Me days without number" (Jeremiah 2:32).

On the other hand, punishment of the women of Israel is described as follows:

"In that day the Lord will *take away the beauty of* their anklets, headbands, crescent ornaments, dangling earrings, bracelets, veils, headdresses, ankle chains, sashes, perfume boxes, amulets, finger rings, nose rings, festal robes, outer tunics, cloaks, money purses, hand mirrors, undergarments, turbans and veils. Now it will come about that instead of sweet perfume there will be putrefaction; instead of a belt, a rope; instead of well-set hair, a plucked-out scalp; instead of fine clothes, a donning of sackcloth; and branding instead of beauty" (Isaiah 3:18-24).

The Father takes these things away from women as a *punishment*. To similarly strip women of things that make them feel beautiful is to penalize them, to even cause them to appear unattractive.

This is the opposite of what the Father promises to do with His bride. If Abba adorns His bride in this way, we should not seek to strip women of the very things He says He will bless His bride with.

These verses teach women not to put their *trust* in outward apparel, but to put it in the beauty of having a pure heart. Outer apparel is not to be a *primary emphasis*. However, making oneself more attractive is certainly acceptable in the Father's eyes.

Within reason, women should feel free to wear, or not to wear, makeup and jewelry.

Ephesians 5:23-33—

"Wives, be subject to your own husbands, as to the Lord. For the husband is the head of the wife, as Messiah also is the head of the church, He Himself being the Savior of the body. But as the church is subject to Messiah, so also the wives ought to be to their husbands in everything.

"Husbands, love your wives, just as Messiah also loved the church and gave Himself up for her, so that He might sanctify her, having cleansed her by the washing of water with the word, that He might present to Himself the church in all her glory, having no spot or wrinkle or any such thing; but that she would be holy and blameless.

"So husbands ought also to love their own wives as their own bodies. He who loves his own wife loves himself; for no one ever hated his own flesh, but nourishes and cherishes it, just as Messiah also does the church, because we are members of His body.

"For this reason a man shall leave his father and mother and shall be joined to his wife, and the two shall become one flesh.

"This mystery is great; but I am speaking with reference to Messiah and the church. Nevertheless, each individual among you also is to love his own wife even as himself, and the wife must see to it that she respects her husband."

Genesis 2:24 says a man is to leave father and mother and "cleave" to his wife. Thus, His mother is no longer the primary woman in his life. This natural process is a final "cutting of the cord" if you will. It is time for the wife to take her place with the man.

Paul also instructs the wives to "submit" to their

husbands, to be in subjection to them.[30]   For this cause they were created, meaning, it is time for the woman to become a godly *k'negdo ezer* to her mate.

However, we note that in the previous verse, Paul told *everyone* to "be subject to one another in the fear of Messiah" (verse 5:21).   And in Galatians 3:28, he said "there is neither Jew nor Greek, neither slave nor free man, neither male nor female; for you are all one in Messiah Yeshua."

We must remember to be balanced in our ideas of female submission. We must remember that the idea of submission speaks of her *choosing* to come alongside her mate to help.

In his letter to the Ephesians, Paul is establishing order in the home. He is saying that the husband is the head/source. He tells wives not to hold themselves above their husbands, and he tells the husbands to love their wives in a sacrificial way. He encourages the men to arise as spiritual leaders in the home—to be the ones who sanctify their wives by washing them with the water of the Word.

One excellent way for a loving husband to "wash" his wife in our day is to have him read the Word to his wife at night before they go to sleep.

Do this men, and watch her heart melt!

---

30 *Strong's* word # G5293.

Ten

Heads and Coverings

*F*ew portions of Scripture have provoked as much discussion as have Paul's discourse on the problems plaguing the people of Corinth.

He wrote to them in response to specific questions they had asked of him, thus we see him addressing their particular situation in his letter:

"But I want you to understand that Messiah is the head of every man, and the man is the head of a woman, and God is the head of Messiah. Every man who has something on his head while praying or prophesying disgraces his head. But every woman who has her head uncovered while praying or prophesying disgraces her head, for she is one and the same as the woman whose head is shaved. For if a woman does not cover her head, let her also have her hair cut off; but if it is disgraceful for a woman to have her hair cut off or her head shaved, let her cover her head. For a man ought not to have his head covered, since he is the image and glory of God; but the woman is the glory of man. For man does not originate from woman, but woman from man, for indeed man was not created for the woman's sake, but woman for the man's sake. Therefore the woman ought to have a symbol of authority on her head, because of the angels. However, in the Lord, neither is woman independent of man, nor is man independent of woman. For as the woman originates from the man, so also the man has his birth through the woman; and all things originate from God. Judge for yourselves: is it proper for a woman to pray to God with her head uncovered? Does not even nature itself teach you that if a man has long hair, it is a dishonor to him, but if a woman has long hair, it is a glory to her? For her hair is given to her for a covering. But if one is inclined to be contentious, we have no other practice, nor have the churches of God" (1 Corinthians 11:3-16).

Boss or Source?

In these verses Paul first addresses "headship," then "covering" one's head. When speaking of the man being the "head" of woman, he used the Greek word *kephale* (*kef-ah-lay*), which can mean "head," as in part of one's body, however, it also was used to mean foremost, as in position.

John Bristow argues that *kephale* can mean a person's head, but that the word was "never used to mean 'leader' or 'boss' or 'chief' or 'ruler.'" He says it also is a military term, meaning "one who leads," or "went before the troops, the leader in the sense of being...the first into battle" (pp 35-37).

Bristow explains that two Greek words can be translated into the one English word, *head*. One, *arche*, (ar-kay) means "boss," and the other, *kephale*, means head as in the "the first soldier into battle."

Unfortunately, an English-speaking person who reads that "the husband is head of his wife" will normally conclude that this means the husband is to *rule* over, or be the boss over, his wife.

"This is what Aristotle taught and what most Hellenized people thought. The husband was an *arche* to his wife, [meaning] head of the household and ruler over his family" says Bristow.

Exploring the difference in these words, Bristow examines the *Septuagint*, a Greek translation of the Hebrew Old Testament, in use at the time of Paul, and he says of his findings:

"In Hebrew, just as in English, one word means both 'physical head' and 'ruler.' The word is *rosh*.

"If *arche* and *kephale*...could be used interchangeably, then when the[y]...came to the Hebrew word *rosh*, they could have used either Greek word.... However, ...When *rosh* meant 'physical head' [or] the first soldier leading others into battle, they... translated it *kephale*. But when *rosh* meant 'chief' or 'ruler,' they translated it *arche* or some form of that word. Every time, this distinction was preserved....

"[Some assume]...the word...Paul used also carried the figurative meaning of 'boss' or 'ruler.' Paul in fact took great care *not* to say that" (pages 36-38).

Others join Barstow in his conclusion that *kephale* means head, as in *headwaters of a river*, or *source*.[31]

We see that the subject is creation by connecting verses 11:3, 8, and 11: "Understand that Christ is the *source* of every man, and the man is the *source* of a woman, and God is the *source* of Christ....For man does not *originate* from woman, but woman from man; for indeed man was not *created* for the woman's sake, but woman for the man's sake."

---

31 *Ibid.* P 35; and, *Why Not Women?* by Loren Cunningham, David J. Hamilton, Janice Rogers YWAM Publishing, Seattle, WA. 2001, p 163.

While Paul surely believed in the headship of the husband, let us remember that many of the people had pagan backgrounds, and he had to correct their wrong thinking. Thus he affirms that man *is* the *source* for woman, even as our God is the *source* for man. He also counters the false Greco claim that woman was not descended from man, but from a sow, a donkey, or some other despised animal.[32]

Paul wisely points out that, although the first woman came from man, since then, all men have been born of women. Thus, he counters the claims that man was superior, and that woman came first.

The apostle begins his discourse by refuting pagan teachings, and he proceeds to teach "creation order" to a people who did not have a proper understanding of that order. He was not telling men to become "bosses" over their wives. He knew that Yeshua won our hearts, not by rule and domination, but by true self-sacrificing love. Paul wanted us to follow that godly pattern.

Veiling Man

Paul next spoke of a man having "something on his head while praying or prophesying," and he said that such coverings "disgrace" the man's head.

The Greek word being translated "cover" alludes to something that hangs down and covers wholly, like a veil.[33] Here, Paul may have been refuting an effeminate male custom, for he concludes the matter by calling them "customs" (verse 11:16).

In addition to female prostitutes, Corinth had a problem with male prostitutes, and with homosexuality. Paul may have been speaking against men identifying themselves in this way.

---

32 *Why Not Women?* Cunningham, Hamilton, Rogers, p 158.
33 *Strong's* word # G2619.

We know that Paul upheld the Law—on the basis that Messiah Yeshua had been sacrificed for us.[34] And he surely knew that YHVH had commanded His priests *not* to "uncover their heads," but to *wear a "turban"* (Leviticus 21:10; Exodus 28:4).

Thus, Paul's comment would not be a blanket condemnation of men covering their heads, for in certain cases it was commanded. As Bristow says, "For Jews, worshiping without one's head covered was regarded with stern disapproval....They believed the *Shekhinah*, the glory and radiance of the Almighty, surrounds the worshiper and rests upon the man and woman who please God. Therefore, it was regarded as an act of reverence and humility for a person to wear a head covering during worship, just as Moses wore a veil after descending Mount Sinai."

However, some feel Paul was speaking against wearing the *taleet*, the Jewish prayer shawl (which hangs down when placed over the head in prayer). They say wearing it indicated that the head/ source (of power) of the wearer was Moses, and not the *Moshiach*.

Paul may have spoken against making unnecessary demands of new converts, because he wanted the Holy Spirit alone to convict the people.

The Taleet

Others believe the *taleet* replaced the fringed cloak -type garment Israelite men traditionally wore, and that it was regarded as their required garment with fringes, or *tzit tzit* on the corners (Numbers 15:38). And thus, Paul would *not* have spoken against it.

Whatever the problem was, Paul admonished the people not be "contentious" about such "customs."

---

34 See Acts 16:1-3; 18:18; 20:16; 21:21-26; 24:14; 25:8; 28:17-18 ; Rom 7:12,14,22;1 Cor 5:7; 1 Tim 1:8; 2 Tim 3:16-17;

Head Coverings for Women

There is no verse in Scripture that commands a woman to "cover her head." Therefore, Paul had to have been addressing traditions.

Jewish tradition of the day called for women to cover their heads, or to bind up their hair by braiding. A married Jewish woman would not allow her hair to fall around her for everyone to see. It was thought to be her "glory," to be seen only by her husband. To let one's hair fall loosely was unseemly. It might be compared today to taking off one's wedding band, or wearing revealing clothes. When uncovered or loose, hair was thought to send a signal that you were "available."

Corinthian prostitutes, who *were available,* did not cover their heads nor braid their hair, but instead cut their hair short, or even shaved their heads.

In this clash of customs, Paul seems to be opting for the more modest Jewish tradition, and votes against shaved heads, calling the look unnatural. Surely he did not want the women of the congregation to appear to be one with the prostitutes.

Veils In The Old Covenant

We see in Scripture instances of women having their heads covered. For example, if a husband suspected that his wife was committing adultery or fornication, he would go to the priest, who would then inquire of the woman. The priest would "then have the woman stand before YHVH and let the hair of the woman's head go loose, and place the grain offering of memorial in her hands, which is the grain offering of jealousy, and in the hand of the priest is to be the water of bitterness that brings a curse" (Numbers 5:18).

The Historian Josephus believed that if guilty, the woman contracted "dropsy," and one form of dropsy causes swelling of the head. If she did contract a disease that affected the hair, such as leprosy, her hair may have turned white, or fallen out. And the guilty woman would be uncovered for all to see. [35]

Next, when Rebekah first saw Isaac she asked, "'Who is that man walking in the field to meet us?' The servant said, 'He is my master.' Then she took her veil and covered herself." And "Isaac brought her into his mother Sarah's tent, and he took Rebekah, and she became his wife" (Genesis 24:65-67).

Rebekah had already agreed to be betrothed to Isaac, which means she was as a married woman. Yet, she is uncovered in the presence of Isaac's servant. Thus it appears that what we see in this case is an example of a woman veiling herself in the presence of her bridegroom.

Leah similarly veiled herself at her wedding, and thus fooled Jacob with a veil that apparently even covered her face (Genesis 29:23-30).

Finally, when Ruth lay at the feet of Boaz, he said to her, "Bring me the *veil* that thou hast..." (Ruth 3:15, KJV). Or, "Give me the *cloak* that is on you and hold it" (NASB). In this garment, Boaz put "six measures of barley," which was enough to feed both Ruth and her mother-in-law, Naomi (Ruth 3:15-17).

Ruth's garment may have been a large head covering, a cloak with a "hood," or a wrap with sufficient material to cover her hair. Whatever it was, some assume that based on these verses, all Israelite women covered their hair. If so, why?

---

35 *Old Diseases and their Modern Definitions:* Dropsy, Hydrocephalus, www.geocities.com/Heartland/Hills/2840/diseases.html; also see Lectures on Homœopathic Materia Medica by James Tyler Kent, M.D., www.homeoint.org/books3/kentmm/pho-ac.htm; *Notes on Numbers* by Dr. Thomas L. Constable, 2004 Edition, pp 15-16: www.soniclight.com.

The people did not always have access to running water and would want to keep sand and dirt out of their hair. Clean hair was probably a luxury. Even those who are opposed to having to cover their heads would probably do so if they had to live in a dusty nomadic environment. Men also tend to cover their heads in such surroundings.

A Sign of Respect

Woman with hair fastened up. Brussels, Royal Museum of Art and History. Barbara McManus 1988

The custom of covering the head may have been born of necessity, but to some, it was regarded as a sign of respect. However, some tried to legislate it. For according to the *Mishnah*, if a man other than the husband or intimate family member saw a woman's unbound hair, the husband then had legal grounds for divorce.

We can possibly see a reflection of this attitude in that the woman who wiped Yeshua's feet with her exposed hair was called a "sinner" (Luke 7:36-30).

As to whether hair was covered or braided, we note that Peter told believing wives to prefer having a "quiet spirit" to having "braided" hair (1 Peter 3:3-5). Thus we see that at least some of the believing wives of the community "braided" their hair.

In a *Biblical Archaeologist* article, Cynthia Thompson concludes that women in ancient Israel braided their hair as opposed to covering their heads. [36]

---

36 Above graphic from the Thompson article: "Hairstyles, Head-coverings, and St. Paul: Portraits from Roman Corinth," Biblical Archaeologist, June 1988, p. 99. www.gbgm-umc.org

Because of The Angels...

"A woman ought to have a symbol of authority on her head, because of the angels" (verse 11:10).

It has been suggested that Paul wanted women to cover their heads as a testimony to the angels (good and bad)—to show acceptance of the rule of authority established by the Almighty.

It has also been suggested that the head covering worn by the High Priest symbolized authority, meaning he had authority and was under authority. Thus, women should likewise cover their heads, for, like the priests of old, they both have authority, and are under authority.

The King James reads, "For this cause ought the woman to have *power* on her head because of the angels." *Power*, or *authority* (NASB), is translated from the Greek *exousia*, which can mean force, capacity, competency, freedom, mastery, delegated influence, jurisdiction, liberty, right, and strength. [37]

Some suggest the verse means that a woman should have *authority over her own head* at all times —because angels are always present, and therefore, she needs *ever-present power* with which to refute them if necessary.

What is true power and authority?

For one thing, a believing wife has the "power" to sanctify an unbelieving husband, to even make her children holy. She can move her mate from unbelief to faith by her silence. That is true authority.

The purity, reverence, modesty, quiet and gentle spirit of a godly wife carry the weight of true power (1 Corinthians 7:14; 1 Peter 3:1-6). These are the virtues on which women ought to place their primary emphasis.

---

37 *Strong's* word #'s G1849 and 1832.

A woman who chooses to cover her head should realize that her choice will make a statement that will draw attention to herself. And, to cover one's head if one is devoid of the traits of a good wife will send conflicting signals to the outside world. On the other hand, those who honestly feel the Holy Spirit is leading them to cover their heads should not be intimidated by the opinions of mortal men.

Judge For Yourselves...

With these many seemingly conflicting opinions, what are we to conclude?

Our God wants us to worship Him in spirit and truth, however, we must realize that our God is also a God of rule and order.

Concerning this most difficult subject, we see that veiled men, exposed heads, and short hair did not seem indecent to the Corinthian mind, but were unacceptable to the Jewish mind.

These conflicting traditions posed a problem for the Corinthian congregation, and they have posed a problem for all the believing congregations that have followed after them.

Nonetheless, Paul essentially summed up his discourse with the words, *"Judge for yourselves..."*

We suggest that the same rule apply to the people of our day. We also suggest that morality cannot be mandated, for Abba is not looking for robots. Therefore, if having a woman cover her head is a sign that she accepts the Father's divine order, then that conviction must first be written on *her* heart. For our Messiah instructs us to be a people who first "wash the inside of the cup" (Matthew 23:26).

These traditions cannot be legislated by men, no matter how well meaning might be their intentions.

Eleven

Spiritual Coverings

*T*he Christian teaching that all women must be spiritually "covered" by a male, meaning to be under "male headship," is essentially based on 1 Corinthians 11. And the women we listed earlier do appear to have been working in harmony with the men. However, for the sake of balance, we again note that Deborah's instructions did not come from her husband, nor Barak, but from the Almighty Himself (Judges 4). Moreover, the Angel did not first go to Mary's father, nor to her betrothed, Joseph. Instead, he made his offer directly to Mary, and she accepted, without consulting with mortal men.

Women today must have the same freedom to hear the voice of the Spirit. And they must realize that they are called to work *with* man.

We must have headship, for without it we will not have direction. Moreover, man is the established head of the house and must be recognized as such. However, his headship is a call to *servanthood*.

We must not view headship as a matter of women having to submit to male authority, but of women coming alongside men to assist them in the establishment of the kingdom. The married woman works with her husband, and unmarried women and widows work with the males the Father places in their lives.

Male headship is a subject that has been clouded with much misunderstanding and abuse. However, we are warned not to be like the heathen and lord position over others: "You know that the rulers of the Gentiles lord it over them; their great men exercise authority over them. But it is not this way among you, but whoever wishes to become great among you shall be your servant and whoever wishes to be first among you shall be slave of all. For even the Son of Man did not come to be served, but to serve, and to give His life a ransom for many" (Mark 10:42-45).

The issue is not one of headship, but servanthood.

Spiritual Applications

Paul addressed actual problems in his letter to the Corinthians; however, we can also find allegorical truths about "coverings," for they are spoken of by both Isaiah and King David:

"Woe to the rebellious children, saith YHVH, that take counsel, but not of me; and that *cover with a covering, but not of my spirit*, that they may add sin to sin" (Isaiah 30:1, KJV). And, "... O YHVH my God, thou art very great; thou art clothed with honour and majesty. Who *coverest thyself with light as with a garment:* who stretchest out the heavens like a curtain" (Psalm 104:1-2, KJV).

In these verses we see that true covering is not found in men or materials, but that our God is covered in honor, majesty, and light, and He alone is our true "covering."

In 1 Corinthians 11:3-4, Paul tells us that every man who prays or prophesies with his head covered dishonors his head, meaning the Messiah.

Metaphorically, if a man hides, or "covers," his testimony about the Messiah, so that Abba's light cannot be seen in him, he dishonors the Messiah. For we are not to cover our light, but to let it shine (Matthew 5:14-16).

In 1 Corinthians 11:5, Paul says that a women praying or prophesying with her head *uncovered*, dishonors her head, and that a married woman's head is her husband.

Our words can both "cover" and "uncover" others; they have the power to produce blessing or curse. It is as James reveals: the tongue is a small part of the body, yet it can set a forest aflame. In it lies a world of iniquity that can defile the entire body, and even set on fire the course of our life (James 3:5-6).

Wicked people often try to "cover" others with wicked words. King David said, "O God...thou hast *covered* my head in the day of battle...As for the head of those that compass me about, let the mischief of their own lips *cover* them" (Psalm 140:7,9, KJV).

In our call to be an *ezer k'negdo,* a true help meet, we are to "cover" our husbands with the words of our mouths, through prayer, intercession, and through encouraging words spoken directly to them.

If a woman does not confess truth and blessing over her mate, she in essence "uncovers her head." She is not being a helper to him, she is not bringing him "help from the heavenlies," nor spiritual backup from Zion (Psalm 20:2).

If a wife tears her husband down with mean or unkind words or speaks negatively about him, she may find that in her "day of battle" she herself may not be covered by the Lord.

If a woman degrades her husband, especially in public, she uncovers her head. She brings public shame to him and to her Messiah.

Wives should first seek to cover their husband's weaknesses, and not to "uncover" them. Noah's son, Ham, "uncovered" Noah, and it brought a serious curse to his life (Genesis 9:20-27).

Similarly, when we discover nakedness in our mate, we must first seek to cover it—meaning to first attend to it in private (Matthew 18:15-17).[38]

Pure Tradition

Again, we note that Paul concludes his discourse on the topic of coverings by warning us against being "contentious" about the matter (1 Corinthians 11:16). He seems to reason that these are customs and not ordinances. We conclude the same.

In the Messianic world, some men choose to wear a *kippah* (head covering) and some choose not to.

Similarly, some women choose to cover their heads, and others choose not to.

Those who walk among us with properly covered heads should be honored among us—as should those who choose not to cover their heads.

Even if the custom of women covering their heads is rooted solely in Jewish tradition, or in a more ancient custom of ancient Israel, it is nonetheless an essentially honorable tradition. It is one that speaks of honoring the Father's order in the home.

---

38 The germ of this allegorical interpretation about coverings came from the article, *What Does the Bible Say About "Head Coverings?"*, www.bible.com/answers/acoverin.html. The article is from the book, *Neither Male Nor Female* by Dr. Betty Miller. Christ Unlimited Ministries, Inc. 2003. We gratefully acknowledge Dr. Miller's contribution to our understanding.

Twelve

Leftovers

*W*omen the world over are known for cooking up something surprisingly good from left-overs. Therefore, we offer the following leftover tidbits in hopes that they will be used to feed and nurture.

Angel's and Female Assignments

The angels in Heaven surely must know the will of the Father concerning women, and we repeatedly see them giving directions to women that called for bold acts of faith on their part.

Mary, the mother of Messiah Yeshua, had to take a giant leap of faith and believe that without the help of a man, and by the Spirit, she was actually going to give birth to the Messiah.

In her old age, Elizabeth believed that she was going to give birth to the one who would declare the coming of the Messiah. In faith, she became the mother of John the Baptist.

Mary Magdalene had to believe and to boldly

proclaim to the apostles that the Messiah had been resurrected and was alive in a glorified Body.

Messiah Yeshua and Women

Messiah Yeshua often spoke of women in His parables. He spoke of the joy of birth—an honor that the Father bestowed on women alone (John 16:21). He spoke of women going after that which was lost, which speaks of her caring nature.[39]

Women welcomed Him (Luke 10:38). A woman was the first to recognize Him for the truth of who He was, and thus anointed Him (Luke 7:37-44). Women faithfully followed and supported Messiah Yeshua.[40]

Touching Yeshua's Tzit Tzit

In Matthew 9:20-22 we read of a woman who had been suffering from a hemorrhage for twelve years. In faith believing, she touched the "fringe of His cloak," and when she did, Yeshua turned to her and said, "Daughter, take courage; your faith has made you well." At once the woman was made well.

This act shows much more than the wonderful belief that touching the Master would bring healing. Touching a man was forbidden in ancient Israel. A woman would especially avoid "desecrating" a man's *tzit tzit*, meaning the mandated "fringes" found on his garment. For these signified that he was "set apart" to the Almighty.[41] This bold act reveals that she believed that Yeshua would have mercy on her as a woman. He would not be repelled at her touch, but would embrace it as a sign of faith on her part.

When seated at a table, we again see a woman

---

39 Luke 7:44; 8:43-50; 13:21; 15:8.
40 Matthew 15:28; 27:55; Mark 7:25; 5:34; 14:3,9; 15:41; Luke 8:2-5; 23:27,49,55; 24:10,22-24; John 4:7-42; 14:9-21; 19:25
41 See Num 15:38; Deu 22:12; Mat 9:20; 14:36; Mark 6:56; Luke 8:44.

touching the Messiah. When she anointed Him, some men complained about her. But The *Anointed One (Moshiach)* asked, "Why do you bother the woman? For she has done a good deed to Me." And He commanded that the story of the woman's good deed be told throughout the world (Matthew 26:6-13).

The Disciples and Women

The disciples also encouraged the women among them. Peter pointed out a last-days promise that supported the women who were working with them. The Prophet Joel first said it, and Peter later affirmed it: "'It shall be in the last days,' God says, 'that I will pour forth of my spirit on all mankind; and your sons and your daughters shall prophesy, and your young men shall see visions, and your old men shall dream dreams; even on my bondslaves, both men and women, I will in those days pour forth of my spirit and they shall prophesy" (Acts 2:17-18; Joel 2:28).

Virgins and Israel

Israel is described as a "virgin." Our God cries out to us, *"Return, O virgin of Israel"* (Jeremiah 31:21).

Believers who await the Messiah's return are likened to a betrothed virgin: "I betrothed you to one husband, so that to Messiah I might present you as a pure virgin" (2 Corinthians 11:2).

Heaven itself is described as ten virgins: "The kingdom of heaven will be like ten virgins, who took their lamps and went out to meet the bridegroom..." (Matthew 25:1-12).

Virgins depict purity. When betrothed, they portray the idea of having a single eye for their beloved.

The young maidens of a pure Israel epitomize all that Israel's kingdom is called to be. They tend to be concerned only about the things of the Lord (1 Corinthians 7:34). How then, can we knowingly silence their pure voice? How can we be so foolish as to not have them speak their pure words to us?

Widows and Israel

Our God loves, cares for, and protects the orphan and the widow; and He repeatedly warns us not to "oppress" them (Exodus 22:22; Deuteronomy 27:19; Isaiah 1:17; Jeremiah 7:6).

James tells us that, "Pure and undefiled religion in the sight of our God and Father is this: to visit orphans and widows in their distress, and to keep oneself unstained by the world" (James 1:27).

How can we oppress the widow and not allow her to freely speak to the people? Will our God allow such oppression to go unpunished?

Young Mothers and Seasons

Digressing for a moment, we note that Solomon said, "To every thing there is a season, and a time to every purpose under the heaven" (Ecclesiastes 3:1, KJV). And that, "There is an appointed time for everything. And there is a time for every event under heaven—*a time to give birth* and a time to die; a time to plant and a time to uproot what is planted" (Ecclesiastes 3:3).

There is a time in life when women are to concern themselves with giving birth and raising a family.

Older women know that once passed, that season feels like it was all too short. Many women wish they could return to those days and do a better job, but opportunities with the little ones are forever gone.

To properly raise a family is time consuming, and sometimes young mothers feel they do not have time to devote to "ministry." However, there is no more important ministry than raising our children. Abraham was especially chosen because Abba knew that he would teach his children about his faith (Genesis 18:18).

The window of opportunity in which we might raise our children closes all too soon. When it is open, it is to be enjoyed to the utmost. These times are like spring and summer months in our lives, and soon enough, fall and winter come.

Nothing is ever as sweet as the season of raising children. It is meant to be a season of joy and laughter. The name of Abraham's chosen heir was *Isaac*, which means *laughter*, so when Sarah was raising their child, there was "laughter" in their tent.

If you have been blessed with an opportunity to raise little ones, let lots of laughter likewise be found in your tent. Raise your chosen seed in delight. Part of the future of the kingdom has been placed in your hands. So enjoy the season. Have fun. Delight in your inheritance. The rest of the world can wait!

Feminine Zion

Returning to our listing of feminine depiction in Scripture, we note that Zion represents the epitome of all that we hope for as Believers. It represents the pinnacle of our faith, and Zion is described as a "Daughter."

"Say to the daughter of Zion, 'Behold your king is coming to you, gentle, and mounted on a donkey, even on a colt, the foal of a beast of burden.'"

"Fear not, daughter of Zion; Behold, your king is coming, seated on a donkey's colt" (Matthew 21:5; John 12:15).

In the same vein, the bride, the New Jerusalem, is described in feminine terms. John says of her, "I saw

the holy city, new Jerusalem, coming down out of
heaven from God, made ready as a bride adorned for
her husband" (Revelation 21:2).

Surely the Holy One of Israel loves the women that
He created. The culmination of His creation is even
described in feminine terms.

Thirteen

*First Direction—
Then Correction*

Torah is a feminine word that speaks of direction. It is derived from *yarah*, a root word that speaks of flowing as water, of an arrow, of pointing out, and thus, instruction.[42]

Torah teachings are meant to flow as water. They are meant to cleanse, to refresh, and to restore the heart. They are meant to be like an arrow, and arrows determine *direction*. They hit the *target*. So our first aim as people of the Holy One should be to show love to one another.

We love because the Messiah *first* loved us (1 John 4:19). Love begets love. And love is first established in the heart of a child by the mother. He is offered the milk of kindness and is filled. However, in this last day, the love of many is waxing cold.

---

42 *Strong's* words # H 8451; 3384.

Mamaʼs Torah

Some are leaving their First Love and walking away from Yeshua (Revelation 2:4). This is partly because we have failed to truly show forth His love. We have failed to release the vessels of love among us. We have kept women in shackles of silence. To rectify this situation, we need to send forth arrows that will tenderly pierce hearts.

Bows and Arrows

The husband and wife team are like a bow and arrow. The husband is the strength of the home, and the wife determines its direction. Judah and Ephraim too are likened to a bow and arrow. For YHVH says, "I will bend Judah as My bow, I will fill the bow with Ephraim....YHVH will appear over them, and His arrow will go forth like lightning; and YHVH will blow the trumpet, and march in the storm winds of the south. YHVH of hosts will defend them. They will...drink and be boisterous as with wine....And YHVH their God will save them in that day as the flock of His people; for they are as the stones of a crown, sparkling in His land" (Zechariah 9:13-16).

In this awesome day of redemption of the whole house of Israel, the Father swears that "His arrows will go forth like lightning" (verse 14).

When Judah and Ephraim come together, Judah brings the Instructions, and Ephraim brings the Holy Spirit. Each brings to the table a certain power.

We repeatedly see Ephraim's call as one who determines direction. They are the watchmen who point out the way: "For there will be a day when watchmen on the hills of Ephraim call out, 'Arise, and let us go up to Zion, to YHVH our God'" (Jeremiah 31:6). [43]

---

43 See, Hos 9:8; *Who Is Israel?*, Wootten, "Called to Be Watchmen."

First The Spirit...

Torah teachings are to always be given *in the spirit*. To try to train a son in the commandments without first training him in his mother's teaching, is like trying to send your son off to high school before he ever goes to kindergarten.

Elementary things must come first. Foundations are first laid before we put up walls and roofs. Likewise, we must begin with the spirit of Torah (Mama), if the children of Israel are ever to be equipped to appreciate the details of Torah (Papa).

We need to hear the voice of women in our midst, be they single, married, or widowed. We also need to have men and women walk together in true harmony. Then Torah arrows will be released that go straight to the heart of the matter. Moreover, we need gentleness in both men and women, that we might be like Paul's proverbial "nursing mother who tenderly cares for her own children" (1 Thessalonians 2:7).

The mother's torah verses reveal that writing Torah on man's heart did not begin with the New Covenant, nor with Torah's command to "circumcise" our hearts. Instead it began with the first mother.

True Torah is meant to nurture—if it does not nurture, it is not true Torah. This principle holds true even when teaching people about the Living Torah, Messiah Yeshua.

To follow the established pattern, we must first have Mama's Torah and develop a right heart attitude. Then we will be able to become true sons of the Commandments. Then we will be empowered to become mature sons who are able to take the Land!

Battling Brothers

Our God wants to restore the whole house of Israel, but the "sibling rivalry" of both houses gets in the way. It is deeply rooted in both people groups. Each thinks they are right and the other is wrong.

Those who seek the restoration of all Israel will have to be like a mother who has two sons, both of whom have bad attitudes toward the other.

Our imaginary "Johnny and Joey" story depicts the problem.

Johnny and Joey were brothers, and older Johnny was the type who would pinch his little brother when Mama wasn't looking. He also would tell little Joey that he was "adopted."

"I know," he would say, "they found you under a rock! I was there when they brought you home!!"

This of course would bring Joey to tears. It made him question whether he really "belonged" to the family. It also made him very, very angry. And Joey had a real problem with anger. So, when Johnny taunted him, Joey would in turn hit him really hard with his plastic bat.

One day, while playing in their bedroom, and after going through their usual routine, Johnny jumped on Joey for hitting him.

Fists flying, the two boys fell on the bed. In the fray, Joey's arm got tangled in the cord that went to the lamp sitting on the night table.

This sent the lamp crashing to the floor, which sound coincided with the breaking of the bed frame. All of which caused their mother to come running...

The challenge for our imaginary mother is that when she comes into the room, she must make a judgment call as to what happened. If she blames Joey for something that Johnny did, Johnny will think his mother is a *schnook*, and Joey will think she is *unfair*. To fully settle the dispute, Mama must judge with absolute equity. Anything less will only fuel their ever-smoldering flame.

The same principle holds true for Ephraim and Judah. As we seek to put an end to their ancient family rift, we must use equal weights and measures. For differing measures are an abomination to our God. They even shorten our days.

We are to be a people who speak the truth, and judge with truth, ever seeking peace in our gates. For Messiah Yeshua warns us not to "judge according to appearance, but to judge with righteous judgment" (Deuteronomy 25:13-16; Proverbs 20:10. Zechariah 8:16; John 7:240).

We will have to be like "dedicated parents" if we want to restore all Israel. We will also have to realize that both houses of Israel have been blinded in part, and that both have stumbled over the Sanctuary, who is Messiah Yeshua (Genesis 48:19; Isaiah 8:14; John 2:19-22; Romans 11:25).

Yet both houses are beloved and chosen children of the Father. Therefore, let us be people who seek to repair their age-old breach (Jeremiah 33:23-26; Isaiah 58:12). Let us be to them like mothers who nurture.

Mama's Torah

Fourteen

The Truth About Torah...

We now offer a variety of teachings about true Torah in hopes that they will fill our hearts with freedom in the Messiah and Spirit-filled wisdom from above. May understanding be granted to us that will empower us to run the race, that we might soon find our way home to Zion.

The Father's Covenant—

Moses told the people, "YHVH declared to you His covenant which He commanded you to perform, that is, the Ten Commandments; and He wrote them on two tablets of stone" (Deuteronomy 4:13).

"YHVH's covenant...is the Ten Commandments."

The Father's covenant is simple, even brief. He used its few words to convey to us the essence of His Torah.

The Father's Covenant Tablets were carried by the Levites *in* "the Ark of the Covenant" (Deuteronomy 31:9).

Moses then "commanded the Levites who carried the Ark, saying:

'Take this book of the law and place it *beside* the ark of the covenant of YHVH your God, that it may remain there as a witness..." (Deuteronomy 31:9,26-27).

The book of the law was placed *beside*, or *outside*, the Ark, there to serve as a "witness."

A witness testifies either for, or against, you.

From this we see that Abba's plan is to have the Torah give "testimony" to us about how well we are walking in His simply stated Covenant—which is the Ten Commandments.

The Essence of the Essence

Messiah Yeshua was once asked, "Teacher, which is the greatest commandment?" He answered, "You shall love the LORD your God with all your heart, and with all your soul, and with all your mind. This is the great and foremost commandment. The second is like it, 'You shall love your neighbor as yourself. On these two commandments depend the whole Law and the Prophets" (Matthew 22:36-40).

The Ten Commandments represent the essence of Torah. Yeshua reduced these to their essence when He named the two primary commands. And the common denominator in these two is the word "love."

Thus we see that the essence of Abba's Torah can be reduced to one word: *Love*.

Our "God is Love" (1 John 4:8,16), and the essence of His Torah is "Love."

The Witness of Torah

When we wonder if we properly understand a matter, for guidance we look to the Torah and its companion Writings (meaning the entire Word, Genesis to Revelation).

The written Word clarifies matters and helps us to see if we are walking correctly. The Spirit speaks to us through the written Word: "Thine ears shall hear a word behind thee, saying, This is the way, walk ye in it..." (Isaiah 30:21, KJV).

When we do not understand the spirit of Abba's Law we tend to stumble over the minutia of the Book of the Law. Then the letter of the Law becomes "a testimony against us."

The Law, the entire Word of the Almighty, needs to first be apprehended by the Spirit. This is why we need to be born from above, by the Spirit, and thus be empowered to truly communicate with Him.

Born From Above—And Yet...

We were made to die to the Law through the body of Messiah, so that we might be joined to another, to Him who was raised from the dead, in order that we might bear fruit for God. We have been buried with Messiah through baptism into death, so that as He was raised from the dead through the glory of the Father, so we too might walk in newness of life. In Him, we are born again of an imperishable seed and are a new creation in Messiah Yeshua.[44] And yet...

It is written of the Father's Commandments:

"Keep and do them, for that is your wisdom and understanding in the sight of the peoples." And, "You

---

44 Rom 7:4; 6:4; 1 Pet 1:3,23; Gal 6:15.

shall keep every commandment...so that you may be strong [*chazak*] and go in and possess the land" (Deuteronomy 4:6; 11:8).

As watchmen, we are to "keep," or "*shawmar*," the commandments. We are to hedge about, guard, protect, and attend to them. As new creations in Messiah Yeshua, we are to be circumspect, take heed, mark, look at, observe, preserve, regard, reserve, save, and watch over them.[45]

And we must do this in the Spirit...

Torah and The Holy Spirit

The essence of Torah was first written in flames of fire on tablets of stone by the finger of our God. It was then written with tongues of fire on hearts of flesh by the Spirit of our God.[46]

Shavuot, (Pentecost) speaks of having the spirit of our Father's Covenant brought to life in men's hearts. On a Shavuot day long ago, He gave us His Ten Commandments, and on a Shavuot day many years later, He poured out His Spirit on Messiah Yeshua's disciples.

Hebrew
Sheen

Cloven
Tongues
of
Fire

"*Cloven* tongues" of fire sat on them and they were filled with the Spirit (Acts 2:3-4).[47]

This speaks of the Father putting His seal, or "initial" on them, it being the Hebrew *Sheen*, the first letter in *Shaddai*—the *Almighty*.

Yeshua's disciples were thus marked, clothed from on High, *Spirit empowered* for service (Luke 24:49).

We need that same empowerment. We will not have a true Hebraic restoration without it.

---

45 *Strong's* word # H8104.
46 Jer 31:31-33; Heb 8:8-13; 10:16-17; Acts 2:3; Luke 24:49.
47 *Strong's* word # G1266.

Dead Men Walking

The problem is that we cannot "keep" all of the commandments, and if we break even one of them, we need a "sacrifice." Thus, *apart from our Messiah and His sacrifice in our behalf,* we are but "dead men walking." We have been weighed and found wanting. We spend our days waiting for our execution date, the day we die. Without Yeshua, we are dead in our trespasses because the wages of sin is death.

Thus we approach Torah's precepts as men who have been tried, found guilty, and put to death for our sins. In this way, we are redeemed from the curse of death found in the Law. For we realize that if we were living under the Law, we would have been stoned to death if we were to:

- Strike or curse our father or mother
- Rebel against our parents
- Offer our children to a pagan god
- Murder or kidnap someone
- Allow our ox to kill someone
- Break the Sabbath
- Lead others astray
- Serve other gods
- Play the harlot
- Commit adultery, incest, lie with the same sex, or an animal
- Act as, or consult with, a medium
- Take in vain the Name of the Lord
- Be in an unauthorized place in the Temple [48]

We who hope in Messiah Yeshua can rejoice because we have been raised in newness of life. In Him, we live anew. And in our new life, we *choose* to serve the One who found us guilty in the first place.

---

48 Exo 21:12,16,17; 21:29; 22:19; 31:14, 15; Lev 20:2,11,13,27; 24:16; Num 3:10; 15:35; Deu 13:10; 17:5; 21:21; 22:21; 22:24.

Thus Paul writes that we were "made to die to the Law through the body of Messiah, that we might be joined to another, to Him who was raised from the dead, in order that we might bear fruit for God" (Romans 6:23; 7:4).

Robots or Those Who Choose To Serve?

As born-again Believers we need to bear good fruit, and we need to help bring restoration to the whole house of Israel. We can best do that by walking in the *wisdom* of Torah. However, our walk must reflect our New Covenant redemption in Messiah Yeshua, and be written on hearts by the *Ruach*.[49]

We must realize that Abba does not want us to be obedient because it is mandated that we do so. He wants us to *choose* Him. That is what it means to be part of the "chosen" people: we are *chosen to choose*. "Choose this day whom you will serve, O Israel" (Joshua 24:15).[50]

Abba is not looking for puppets or robots, but for a people who delight to walk in His way. He tells us to "Ask for the ancient paths, where the good way is, and walk in it; and you will find rest for your souls" (Jeremiah 6:16).

He wants us to delight in the Sabbath rest of our Messiah, so He can "make us ride on the heights of the earth," and "feed us with the heritage of Jacob" (Isaiah 58:1-14; Hebrews 4:1,9).

However, we must realize that His many children can be in various stages of learning about His ways. We must not try to force-feed them truths He mercifully shows us, nor be condescending to them. Messiah Yeshua did not treat us that way, but instead came to us in mercy. We must do the same.

49 Jer 31:31-33; Heb 8:10; 10:16.
50 Exo 19:4-6; Deu 4:37; 7:6-8; 10:15; 30:19 Jer 33:23-26; 1 Pet 1:1; 2:9.

Rabbi Paul

Paul loved the Father's Law. He walked in the New Covenant, yet did not speak against Torah, as he is falsely accused of doing. We see this truth in that:

- He circumcised Timothy (Acts 16:1-3).
- He did not teach Believers to forsake Moses (Acts 6:13;18:18; 21:21-26).
- He believed in, even delighted in, God's law (Acts 24:14; Romans 7:22).
- He committed no offense against it (Acts 25:8)
- He said the Law is good—if one uses it lawfully (1 Timothy 1:8; Romans 7:12,14; 2:13).

Paul argued against *Judaizers* who wanted to impose their interpretations of the Law onto the non-Jewish Believers. [51] He declared that legalistic observance does not bring eternal salvation; that comes by being born anew through faith in Messiah Yeshua (Galatians 4:8-11).

Paul warned against the traditions of men. He spoke against men who gathered people to themselves, and thus put their followers in bondage (Colossians 2:8; Galatians 4:17).

The Jerusalem Council ruled that new converts were to obey certain minimal requirements and go to the synagogue where they would hear the words of Torah. They would thus hear the Word, and by the Spirit, be transformed (Acts 15:21; Jeremiah 31:31-33).

Paul understood this principle. He declared that true meaning and fulfillment of the feasts and the Law are found only in the Messiah.

May we be as understanding of Torah as was the little Rabbi from Tarsus.

---

51 Judaizers: Those who try to bring people into conformity with Judaism, especially to adopt rabbinic interpretations of Torah and oral law.

A Latter Day Flood of Words

Messiah Yeshua promised to guide us to the water of life, and to give it to those who thirst without cost.

We are headed toward a city that has a River of Life flowing through it. Thus, the Spirit and the bride beckon to us, saying, *"Come..."* [52]

We long for the River of Life. But the Counterfeiter wants to drown us in a very different river.

Satan is now sending forth a river of death, especially designed to sweep away the woman, Israel.

Revelation 12:15 warns that in the last days, the serpent will pour "water like a river out of his mouth after the woman, so that he might cause her to be swept away with the flood."

Words come out of the mouth.

HaSatan is now sending forth a flood of words.

What kind of words did he use in the past?

- He distorted the Word when he tempted Eve.
- He twisted it when he tried to tempt Messiah.
- He influenced Eve to eat of the "tree of the knowledge of good and evil" (Genesis 2:9-3:24).

Satan always uses a mix of good and evil words.

In our day, people are being swept away from faith in a divine Messiah and converting to Judaism.

This is happening because Ephraim is jealous of Judah (Isaiah 11:13), and as he awakens to the truth of his roots, he is drawn to study Torah. The Twisted One then tries to ensnare him, to keep him from the full truth, for he ever works against our restoration.

We must not be swept away. We must cling to the truth about our Messiah and about His Holy Spirit.

There is a dangerous flood at hand.

There is also a coming glorious River.

Do not be swept away before you get to taste of it.

---

52 Rev 7:17; 21:6; 22:1-2,17.

Fifteen

Time To Give Birth

$\mathcal{T}$he Holy Spirit is often spoken of in "feminine" terms. For example, in the book of Genesis we see the Spirit "brooding" over the face of the waters, ready to give birth to creation. Similarly, Messiah Yeshua depicts Himself as a mother hen, one that is concerned for His Jewish chicks:

"O Jerusalem, Jerusalem," He cries, "City that kills the prophets and stones those sent to her! How often I wanted to gather your children together, just as a hen gathers her brood under her wings, and you would not have it!" (Luke 13:34).

In His longing for His people, Messiah Yeshua takes on a feminine, motherly passion. He also speaks of the *Ruach HaKodesh* in feminine terms. He promises His followers, "I will send you another *comforter*." This speaks of the "the Spirit of truth," the One who guides us into all truth (John 14:16-26).

As Yeshua begins to bring forth those of returning Israel, they are in many ways like newborn babes.

They are children who need to be protected and comforted. Sometimes they need to be "spoon fed."

Like the prodigal in Messiah's parable, wandering Ephraim long ago left their Father's house. In their *diaspora* (dispersion), they too dishonored instructions given years prior. For the Holy One said of Ephraim: "Though I wrote for him ten thousand precepts of My law, they are regarded as a strange thing" (Hosea 8:12).

So it is that these Ephraimite returnees, and their companions, are in some ways Torah-less. They know the Son, the Living Torah, but have believed that the written Torah was abolished.

They now need a new beginning. They need to be taught the eternal truths of Torah, but they absolutely must avoid the legalism often associated with it.

Legalism was a problem once before in Israel—it being the reason that Judah's house was essentially "left desolate" (Luke 13:35).

Nonetheless, Abba wants to have Judah restored, to be returned to his brothers of Israel (Micah 5:2-3). To accomplish this, He wants Ephraim to learn to walk in a way that will provoke Judah to jealousy (Romans 11). This calls for certain changes first to be worked in Ephraim. Thus, Abba wants to send His Spirit to him in a most powerful way. He also wants to assure Ephraim of His love for him, because, when Ephraim is assured of the Father's love for him, he will be better equipped to show forth that love to brother Judah (Jeremiah 31:18-19).

So it is that the Spirit, like a mother, wants to brood over the tender hearts of these returning chosen ones. He wants to breathe life into their dry bones, and to fill them with mercy. Then they will be like their Messiah—a "mother hen" who longs to gather all the chicks of Israel.

Proclaiming the Good Tidings

The women of returning Israel must be encouraged to arise in this hour, for they have much to do to accomplish Israel's full restoration.

The Psalmist speaks of Abba giving a command, and He says that at that time, "The women who proclaim the good tidings are a great host: Kings of armies flee, they flee, and she who remains at home will divide the spoil! When you lie down among the sheepfolds, you are like the wings of a dove covered with silver, and its pinions with glistening gold" (Psalm 68:11-13.

The King James renders the first verse, "The Lord gave the word: great was the company of those that published it."

This company of women are said to be like "the wings of a dove," which indicates that they are a gentle company, filled with the Spirit.

They also are covered with "silver," and have their feathers brushed with "gold." Silver represents redemption and gold symbolizes purity.

This Psalm is primarily about the judgment and deliverance of the Holy One, and the words describe the times in which we live, for both judgment and deliverance now loom large on the horizon.

In the verses above we see a company of women who arise to champion a cause. They are a purified group of women who publish the truth.

May it be granted from on High that we are found among them.

Turning Things Around

Jeremiah spoke of the Father doing a new thing in the earth, and it too involves women.

This weeping prophet declared:

"YHVH has created a new thing in the earth—a woman will encompass a man" (vs 31:22).

This unique promise appears to involves a "role reversal." Instead of a husband "encompassing" his wife, the wife, being of weaker physical nature,[53] "encompasses" her husband.

Thus Jeremiah asks, "How long will you go here and there, O faithless daughter? For the Lord has created a new thing in the earth—a woman will encompass a man. Thus says the Lord of hosts, the God of Israel, 'Once again they will speak this word in the land of Judah and in its cities when I restore their fortunes, "The Lord bless you, O abode of righteousness, O holy hill!"'" (Jeremiah 31:22-23).

This new thing happens when Judah's fortunes are restored, which occurs in the time of the end. It marks a time when the Holy One of Israel will "satisfy the weary ones and refresh everyone who languishes" (Jeremiah 31:25).

In this verse we see a formerly faithless, backsliding daughter who ceases her wandering. "Faithless" is a word often used to describe the people of Ephraim, those formerly of the Northern Kingdom of Israel. It tells the fate of those destined to become a "fullness of the Gentiles" (Jeremiah 3:6-22; Hosea 10:2; Genesis 48:19; Romans 11:25).

At the time of this refreshing, the Father begins a new work in the earth. It has to do with woman *sadab*, or *surrounding* man. This word can mean bring, lead, make, be on every side, besiege, bring again, change, cause to come about, drive, beset return, turn.[54]

It is most often translated as some form of encompass, turn, or about.

---

53 1 Peter 3:7.
54 *Strong's* and *BDB* word # H5437.

Here we see a picture of the women of today. For they need to be about encompassing mankind, turning them around, that they might be able to return to the Garden, to a glorified Zion.

It is surely time for the woman, virgin Israel, to return, and to fully *encompass* her divine bridegroom, Messiah Yeshua.

Jeremiah was told to "Go and proclaim these words toward the north and say, 'Return, faithless Israel,' declares YHVH; I will not look upon you in anger. For I am gracious...[and will not be angry forever. Only acknowledge your iniquity, that you have transgressed against YHVH your God and have scattered your favors to the strangers under every green tree, and you have not obeyed My voice,' declares YHVH" (Jeremiah 3:12-13).

Once we begin this prophesied return, the Father gives us shepherds who seek after His heart, who feed His people on true knowledge and understanding. Moreover, He says, "In those days the house of Judah will walk with the house of Israel, and they will come together from the land of the north to the land that I gave your fathers as an inheritance" (Jeremiah 3:15-18).

Yes women, we who are said to have "led Adam out of the Garden" can perhaps be used to help lead the way back to Zion (Jeremiah 6:16; 50:5).

So let us hearken to the solemn words of Isaiah: "Rise up, you women who are at ease, and hear my voice; give ear to my word, you complacent daughters" (Isaiah 32:9).

Let us not be complacent about the awesome work that is at hand, let us arise and seek to publish and proclaim the truth. Let us work to turn Israel around, to set her feet on the road to Zion!

Sixteen

Nurturing and Restoration

*T*he faith of Abraham needs to be restored to us, as does the pure Torah that our patriarchs faithfully followed. Likewise, the rightful place of woman needs to be restored.

A true understanding of the scriptural role of women will help pave the way for a proper understanding of the role of the *Ruach HaKodesh* in our lives. For it is He who gives direction in our lives (Luke 12:12; John 14:26).

As for the role of women, our God asks an interesting question of the unfaithful Ephraimites:

"To whom would He teach knowledge, and to whom would He interpret the message? Those just weaned from milk? Those just taken from the breast? For He says, 'Order on order, order on order, line on line, line on line, a little here, a little there'" (Isaiah 28:9-10).

 This verse assumes that the child first gets the breast and is weaned from it before he is able to learn about the Word, "line upon line."

Little wonder that we have failed to apprehend the depths of our Father's Word. For both houses of Israel have in essence been a "breastless people." They have not been given, nor been able to freely drink, mother's milk.

We have not really had the milk, nor been weaned. And until we follow that pattern, we will not be able to handle YHVH's truth, "precept upon precept."

Women need to be released, that they might arise and help bring change to this sad situation.

The True Priest and All Israel

The people of Israel are called to be a kingdom of priests. They are called to serve the Almighty.

"'You shall be to Me a kingdom of priests and a holy nation.' These are the words that you shall speak to the sons of Israel" (Exodus 19:6).

This same call is affirmed in the New Covenant:

"You are a chosen race, a royal priesthood, a holy nation, a people for God's own possession, so that you may proclaim the excellencies of Him who has called you out of darkness into His marvelous light; for you once were not a people, but now you are the people of God; you had not received mercy, but now you have received mercy" (1 Peter 2:9-10).[55]

In ancient Israel, the High Priest bore stones on a breastplate; these stones represented all twelve tribes of Israel.

---

55 See Hosea 1-2.

This picture reveals that a true priest will have the burden of *all Israel* on his heart.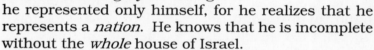

He will take all Israel with him into the Holy of Holies.

A true priest will not appear before the Almighty as though he represented only himself, for he realizes that he represents a *nation*. He knows that he is incomplete without the *whole* house of Israel.

These principles must hold true for all who see what our Father desires to accomplish in this hour. We must cry out for the restoration of the whole house of Israel. We must be like Levites who take their priesthood to heart if we want to minister to the Father and help accomplish His will in the earth.

The Final Hours of The Sixth Day

Many have suggested that we are destined to have "six days," or 6000 years of mankind, and then the "seventh day," the Millennium, and that we are now in the "sixth day," even in the final hours of our saga.

Assuming this is the case, and that we are close to the end of time, we ask:

"What happened on the sixth day of creation?"

The answer is that our God first created Adam, and then He created Eve.

Woman was the last of the Almighty's creation, and perhaps the last to be fully restored to Him.

If so, then perhaps the following is the word of the hour for women everywhere:

If the Almighty created you in His image, to be a deliverer, a champion in Israel, if He sent His Son to redeem and restore women to their rightful place, and if His disciples were working to confirm that restoration, then why do you care about the opinions of unenlightened, fallen men?

Women of Israel, we must learn to sing a song. That song is—

"Though none go with me, still I will follow..."

If women everywhere will begin to believe that the Father has a good plan for their lives, and intends to build them up and not tear them down (Jeremiah 29:11), then we can make a difference in this world.

The world needs to hear the voice of the nurturers. Let us not fail them. Let the voice of mercy be heard in the earth. *Women of Israel, Arise!*

But do not arise thinking you can now do it without the men. No. We have seen the results of having essentially only the male voice be heard in the believing community. We do not need a companion move wherein the female voice is heard without that of the male. That will only make all of us weary.

We must arise as women who realize that men and women, male and female, need each other. Moreover, we must realize that the most "God-like" voice is the voice of men and women united in the Holy One.

May that voice be heard throughout the earth!

Father, we come to you in the mighty Name of our Messiah and we humbly bow before you. We ask You to please empower us by Your Holy Spirit, to help us become the women you want us to be.

We want to come home to Zion.

Please allow that we might be numbered among those who truly were an ezer, as those who truly helped lead the way.

Amen and Amen.

Bibliography

*T*he following is a list of Abbreviations used in
this work.

> *BDB: New Brown-Driver-Briggs-Gesenius Hebrew-
> Aramaic Lexicon*
> *NIV: New International Version Bible*
> *Strong's: Strong's Exhaustive Concordance*

The following is a listing of writings used in the making of
this book.

Bilezekian, Gilbert. *Beyond Sex Roles* Grand Rapids, MI: Baker,
        1985, 1993.
Bristow, John Temple.   *What Paul Really Said About Women*.
        San Francisco, CA: Harper Collins, 1991.
Brown,   Frances. *The New Brown-Driver-Briggs-Gesenius
        Hebrew-Aramaic Lexicon*. Peabody, MA: Hendrickson,
        1979.
Cunningham, Loren; David Joel Hamilton.   *Why Not Women?*
        Seatlle: YWAM Publishing, 2000.
Edersheim, Alfred. *The Life and Times of Jesus the Messiah*.
        Grand Rapids, MI: Eerdman's, 1979.

Edidin, Ben M. *Jewish Customs And Ceremonies*. NY: Hebrew Publishing, 1978.

_____. *Encyclopaedia Judaica, 16 Vols*. Jerusalem: Keter, 1972.

Even-Shushan, Avraham. *New Concordance of the Tanach*. Jerusalem: Sivan, 1983.

Gesenius' Hebrew-Chaldee Lexicon To The Old Testament. Grand Rapids: Baker, 1979.

Green, Jay P. *The Interlinear Bible*, Hebrew, Greek, English. Grand Rapids: Baker, 1979.

Harris, R. Laird, Gleason L. Archer Jr., and Bruce K. Waltke, eds. *Theological Wordbook of the Old Testament, 2 Vols*. Chicago: Moody, 1981.

Hatch, Edwin, and Henry A. Redpath. *Hatch and Redpath Concordance to the Septuagint, 2 Vols*. Grand Rapids: Baker, 1983.

Holladay, William L. Editor. *A Concise Hebrew and Aramaic Lexicon of The Old Testament.* Grand Rapids: Eerdman's, 1971.

Jacob, Cindy. *Women of Destiny*. Ventura, CA: Regal Books, 1998.

Kroeger, Richard Catherine. *I Suffer Not A Woman: Rethinking 1 Timothy 2:11-15 In Light of Ancient Evidence*. Grand Rapids: Baker,1992.

The New Encyclopaedia Britannica, 29 Vols. Chicago: Encyclopedia Britannica, 1985.

New International Version Study Bible. Grand Rapids: Zondervan, 1985, 1995.

Pfeiffer, Charles F., Howard F. Vos, and John Rea, eds. *Wycliffe Bible Encyclopaedia*. Chicago: Moody, 1983.

Scherman, Nosson, and Meir Zlotowitz, eds. *Genesis. ArtScroll Tanach Series*. Brooklyn: Mesorah, 1987.

Spencer, Aida, *Beyond the Curse*. Nashville: Thomas Nelson, 1985.

Strong, James. *The New Strong's Exhaustive Concordance*. Nashville: Thomas Nelson, 1984.

Stern, David H. *Jewish New Testament Commentary*. Clarksville, MD: Jewish New Testament Publications, 1995.

Unger, Merrill F. *Unger's Bible Dictionary*. Chicago: Moody, 1974, 1996.

Vaughn, Curtis, ed. *26 Translations of the Holy Bible*. Atlanta: Mathis, 1985.

Vincent, Marvin R. *Vincent's Word Studies of the New Testament.* McLean, VA: MacDonald.

Vine, W.E. *The Expanded Vine's Expository Dictionary of New Testament Words.* Minneapolis: Bethany, 1984.

Webster's Third New International Dictionary, 3 Vols. Chicago: Encyclopedia Britannica, 1981.

Whiston, William, trs. *The Works of Flavius Josephus, 4 Vols.* Grand Rapids: Baker, 1974.

Wilson, William. *Wilson's Old Testament Word Studies, Unabridged Edition.* McLean, VA: MacDonald.

Wootten, Angus. *Restoring Israel's Kingdom.* Saint Cloud, FL: Key of David, 2000.

Wootten, Batya Ruth. *Ephraim and Judah: Israel Revealed* Saint Cloud: Key of David, 2002.

_____. *Who Is Israel?* Saint Cloud: Key of David, 1998, 2000, 2003.

_____. *Israel's Feasts and their Fullness*, Saint Cloud: Key of David. 2002

Wuest, Kenneth S. *Weust's Word Studies From the Greek New Testament.* Grand Rapids: Eerdman's, 1981.

Mama's Torah

Study Helps

$\mathcal{T}$he following charts, maps, and lists are presented to help the student better understand both women and Israel.

Recommended Reading

*T*he following books are recommended reading. Each work has something valid to offer.

Beyond Sex Roles. What The Bible Says About A Woman's Place In Church and Family by Gilbert Bilezikian Examines woman's place in the church and family. Includes 53 pages of scholarly endnotes. Second edition, 331 pages, Baker Books, 1985. Also available in Spanish.

Good News for Women: A Biblical Picture of Gender Equality by Rebecca Merrill Groothuis Gives an egalitarian view of marriage and gender equality, examines traditionalist proof texts used to relegate women to a subordinate place in church. 272 pages, Baker Books, 1997.

What Paul Really Said About Women: An Apostle's Liberating Views on Equality in Marriage, Leadership and Love by John Temple Bristow Challenges traditional interpretations of Paul's writings, gives actual meaning of key words. Reveals how the views of pagan philosophers Aristotle, Plato, and Socrates, influenced church understanding. 126 pages, Harper & Row, 1991.

Beyond Sex Roles by Gilbert Bilezekian. A teacher of Biblical Studies at Wheaton College, Bilezekian provides much food for thought for both men and women. Well reasoned and excellent work. 1985, Baker.

I Suffer Not A Woman: Rethinking 1 Timothy 2:11-15 In Light of Ancient Evidence by Richard and Catherine Kroger. This fascinating and well documented study is nonetheless easy to read. Sheds much light on formerly difficult passages. 1992, Baker.

Why Not Women? A Biblical Study of Women in Missions, Ministry, and Leadership by Loren Cunningham, David J. Hamilton, Janice Rogers Examines the place of women in missions, ministry and leadership. Includes a detailed study of women in Scripture and difficult passages relating to women, plus teaching on the original cultures and languages of the Bible. 279 pages, YWAM Publishing, 2001.

Women in the Church: A Biblical Theology of Women in Ministry by Stanley J. Grenz, with Denise Muir Kjesbo The role of women in the church today. Carefully considers biblical, historical, and practical concerns about women and ministry. 284 pages, InterVarsity Press, 1995.

Equal to Serve: Women and Men Working Together Revealing the Gospel Gretchen Gaebelein Hull   Examines Old and New Testament passages about women in the church, home and society. Deals with justice, patriarchy, mutual submission, controversial areas. 302 pages, Baker 1998. (Out of print. Try Amazon.com for used copies.)

Gender and Grace: Love, Work, and Parenting in a Changing World by Mary Stewart Van Leeuwen   Clear, well-reasoned arguments about the part genes, culture and faith play in making us. Explores statistics and traditions. 275 pages, InterVarsity, 1990 (Out of print: Try Amazon).

Women of Destiny by Cindy Jacobs An intercessor and Aglow Board member offers solid scriptural research combined with theological integrity, humor, and personal testimony to lead readers through the taboos of women in the ministry. Very readable. 322 pages. Gospel Light. 1998.

Women: God's Secret Weapon by Ed Silvoso The Fall in Genesis relates to women's ultimate role in defeating Satan. Encourages women to step beyond stereotypical roles and to find healing from hurts. 160 pages. Regal Publishing. 1999.

Neither Male Nor Female by Betty Miller.   84 pages. Christ Unlimited Ministries, Inc. 2003.

The Role of Women in the Assembly by Scott and Jane Diffenderfer Excellent article about women in the assembly. www.messianichome.org, Lebanon, TN.

Women in Ministry by Rav Hollisa Alewine Olive Branch, www.israelnet.tv

Discovering The Heart of A Man by Ken Nair 1992. Companion to the "absolute must read" book listed below.

For the Men: *Discovering The Mind of A Woman The Key To Becoming a Strong and Irresistible Husband* by Ken Nair. Many marriages have been healed and improved based on the wisdom found in the pages of this highly recommended book. Thomas Nelson. 1995.

Women in Scripture

Abigail: 1 Samuel 25-30;
Anna (Hannah): Luke 2:36
Deborah: Judges 4-5
Dorcas (Tabitha): Acts 9:36-39
Elizabeth (mother of John the Baptist): Luke 1
Esther: Esther 1-10
Euodias: Philippians 4:2
Eve: Genesis 1-4; 2 Corinthians 11:3; 1 Timothy 2:13
Hagar: Genesis 16; 21; 25; Galatians 4:24-25
Hannah: 1 Samuel 1- 2
Huldah: 2 Kings 22:14; 2 Chronicles34:22
Jael (Yael):   Judges 4-5
Jezebel: 1 Kings 16-21; 2 Kings 9: Revelation 2:20
Junia: Romans 16:7
Leah: Genesis 29-35; 46; 49
Miriam: Exodus 15:20-21; Numbers 12; Micah 6:4
Mary (Miriam: mother of Yeshua):   Luke 1 & 2
Mary (sister of Martha): Luke 10:39; John 11:1-20
Mary Magdalene: Matthew 27-28; Luke 8:2; John 20
Martha: Luke 10; John 11-12
Naomi: Ruth 1-4
Nympha: Colossians 4:15
Orpah: Ruth 1:4,14
Philip's four daughters: Acts 21:9
Ruth: Ruth 1-4
Phoebe: Romans 16:1-2
Priscilla: Acts 18; Romans 16:3; 1 Corinthians 16
Rachel: Genesis 29-35; Jeremiah 31:15; Matthew 2:18
Rahab: Joshua 2, 6; Matthew 1:5; Hebrews 11:31
Rebekah: Genesis 22-28; 49:31; Romans 9:10
Sarah: Genesis 15-25; Isaiah 51:2; Hebrews 11:11
Syntyche: Philippians 4:2-3
Tabitha (Dorcas): Acts 9:36,40
Wife of Manoah: Judges 13

Glossary of Hebrew Words

- *Abba:* Affectionate term for Father, like Daddy.
- *Brit HaDoshah:* The New [Renewed] Covenant.
- *Kippah:* Skull cap worn by Jews during prayer; the Yiddish term is *yarmulke.*
- *Messiah Yeshua:* Jesus was given the Hebrew name Yeshua when He was born. Christ is from the Greek *Christos*, which is translated from the Hebrew, *Moshiach.* From this word we get *Messiah*, which means *anointed.*
- *Mikvah:* Ritual bath in running water (such as the Jordan River). Baptism.
- *Mishnah:* Code of Jewish oral law
- *Moshiach:*: Anointed One (see Messiah Yeshua)
- *Rav:* Shortened form of Rabbi
- *Ruach HaKodesh: The Spirit Most Holy*
- *Shekhinah:* The visible divine Presence that rested between the cherubim over the Ark's Mercy Seat.
- *Taleet (Talit, Talis)* Prayer shawl with ceremonial fringes (see *Tzit Tzit*) on the four corners.
- *Tanach (Tenach):* Acronym for the Hebrew Bible, consisting of Torah, Prophets, and Writings; from the initial letters of those Hebrew words: *Torah, Nevi'im, Ketuvim. TNK.*
- *Tzit Tzit:* Braided fringes of Numbers 15:38, put on the corners of one's garment.
- *YHVH* The Name of the one true God is comprised of four Hebrew letters: *yod, hey, vav, hey:* יהוה. This Name is often translated as "God" or "Lord," but these are *titles* and not His Name. To indicate His Name, we use the four English letters that most closely resemble those Hebrew letters: YHVH.

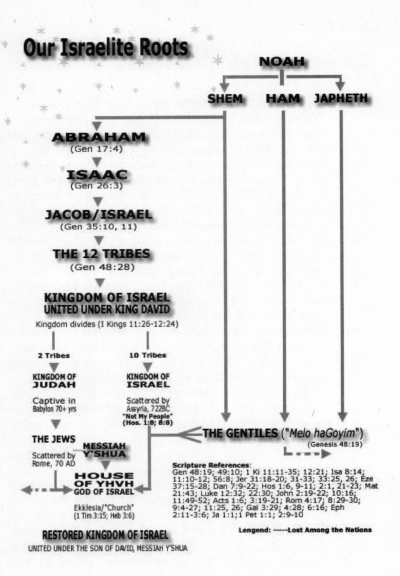

There Are Two Main Branches In The Olive Tree of Israel: Ephraim and Judah

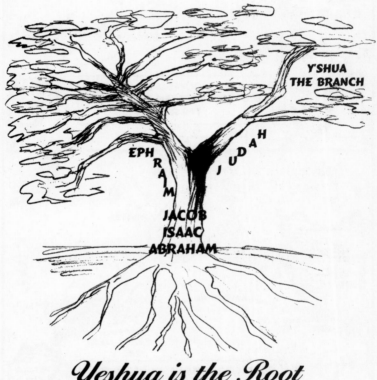

Yeshua is the Root

When the Father first called "Israel" an "*olive tree.*"
He specifically said He was speaking to:
"The house of Israel *and* the house of Judah" (Jeremiah 11:10).
Yeshua said, "*I am the root* and *the offspring* of David."
And, Isaiah calls the Messiah, "The Branch"
(Revelation 22:16; Isaiah 11:1).

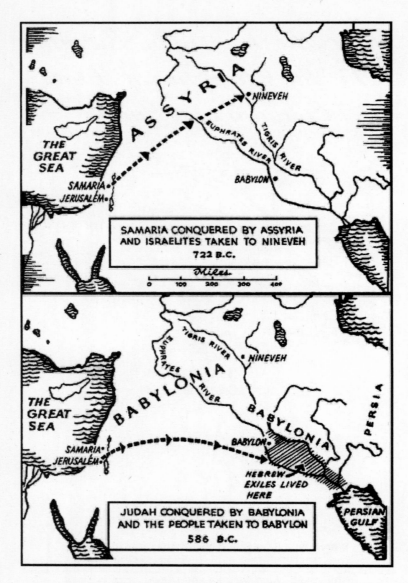

From A Map Book For Bible Students by Frederick L. Fay, page 18,
Old Tappan, NJ: Fleming H. Revell.
Used by permission.

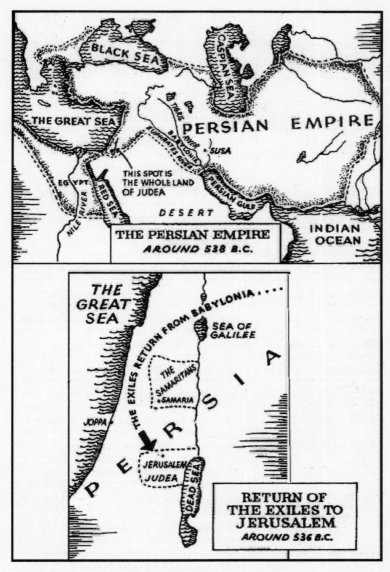

From A Map Book For Bible Students by Frederick L. Fay, page 20,
Old Tappan, NJ: Fleming H. Revell.
Used by permission.

Scripture	Restored Israel Hallmarks
Isaiah 11:13	Ephraim's jealousy departs
Jeremiah 31:18,19	Ephraim repents of his paganism
Isaiah 11:13	Those hostile to Judah are cut off
Isaiah 11:13	Judah ceases to vex Ephraim
Zechariah 10:7	Ephraim becomes like a mighty man
Hosea 11:10	Ephraim comes trembling from the West
Zechariah 10:8,10	Ephraim returns in great numbers
Obadiah 1:18	Jacob becomes a fire, Joseph a flame
Zechariah 9:13	Judah is like a bow, Ephraim the arrow
Jeremiah 3:14; 50:5	Repentant Israel asks for the way to Zion
Jeremiah 50:20	No more iniquity found in Israel
Jeremiah 3:17;16:14	Both forget the Ark and the Exodus
Zechariah 8:3,7,13	Both call Zion The City of Truth
Ezekiel 37:15-28	Two sticks become one nation in the land
Ezekiel 37:24	Ephraim & Judah have one king—Yeshua
Ezekiel 37:23-24	Not defiled with any transgressions
Ezekiel 37:26-27	YHVH's sanctuary is in their midst forever

Until the above verses are completely fulfilled
the Father is still working with both the houses of Israel.
Ephraim and Judah have not been fully reunited—
our unity has been imputed in the Messiah,
but we have not fully implemented that unity.

The Hope of Messianic Israel

Messianic Israel believes Yeshua Ha'Natsree (Jesus of Nazareth) was and is the true Messiah, the Lion of Judah, the Branch Who will fully reunite all Israel; that He died and rose from the dead and lives at the right hand of the Almighty; and according to the ancient Holy Scriptures, Yeshua is YHVH Elohim appearing in the flesh, as Yeshua demonstrated in Himself (Deu 18:18-19; John 8:58; 10:33; Mat 12:6-8; 9:35; 15:31; Isa 11; 53; Micah 5:2-4; Luke 24:46; Isa 8:14; John 2:22; Acts 3:15-17; Heb 13:20; 1 John 4:2; 2 John 1:7; Rev 5:5; John 1:1).

We believe we are made righteous in Messiah Yeshua. (He is the heart of Abraham's unconditional covenant.) The sign of the New Covenant is circumcision of the heart, which leads to confession, salvation, faith, grace, and to good works in Messiah. The conditional Mosaic covenant presents the eternal truths of Torah (YHVH's teaching and instructions) to His people, the hearing of which brings about blessing or curse (respond and be blessed, disobey and lack). In the New Covenant, Yeshua's Law is to be written on our hearts by the Spirit (Rom 4:13-16; 5:2; 10:10; 1 Pet 1:19; 2 Cor 5:21; Gal 3:16,29; Titus 3:5; Heb 10:38; 1 John 1:9; Eph 2:8; James 2:14; Deu 28; Ezek 36:26; Jer 31:31-33; Heb 10:16; Gal 2:16; John 5:46; 10;30; 14:2; 15:10).

We desire to fully reunite the olive tree of Israel, both branches, Ephraim and Judah, into one, redeemed, nation of Israel—through Messiah Yeshua. We seek to arouse Ephraim from obscurity, and by example, to awaken Judah to the Messiah, and thus to hasten both Yeshua's return to Earth and the restoration of the kingdom to Israel (Mat 6:10; 12:25; 21:43; 24:43; Luke 22:29-30; Mark 13:34; Luke 22:29-30; 2 Chr 11:4; Eze 37:15-28; Jer 11:10,16; 2:18,21; Rom 11:17,24; Eph 2:11-22; Acts 1:6).

We deem the Jewish people to be the identifiable representatives and offspring of Judah and "the children of Israel, his companions," and non-Jewish followers of the Messiah from all nations have been, up to now, the unidentifiable representatives and offspring of Ephraim and "all the house of Israel, his companions" (Gen 48:19; Hosea 1-2; 5:3; Eze 37:16; Jer 31:6-9; Gen 15:2-5; 26:3; 28:4; Heb 11:9; Isa 56:3,6-8; Eph 2:11-22).

We affirm that the Jewish people have been kept identifiable as seed of the patriarch Jacob, YHVH's covenant people, to preserve His Holy Torah (Law), Feasts, and Sabbath; that the salvation of the Jewish people through their acceptance of Messiah Yeshua, will be the crowning act of mankind's redemption, and is necessary for the restoration of Israel's kingdom. Further, the Father plans that Ephraim, they being the "wild olive branch," stimulate Judah to want what they have; they are called to walk in a way that will make Judah jealous of their relationship with the God of Israel (Gen 48:19; Isa 11:13; 37:31,32; Zec 2:12; Eze 37:15-28; Hosea 1:7; Rom 10:19; 11:11,14; Mat 23:39).

We believe that the non-Jewish followers of Yeshua are predominantly returning Ephraim, those who were once among the Gentiles/*Goyim*/Nations as "LoAmi,"or "Not a people," but have now been restored to the commonwealth of Israel through their covenant with Israel's Messiah; that, they are no more Gentiles/*Goyim*/of the Nations, but fulfill the promised restoration of uprooted Ephraim, and Jacob's prophecy that Ephraim would become "melo hagoyim," the "fullness of the Gentiles/Goyim/ Nations." As Ephraim, they have been kept in mystery until recently, being used to preserve the testimony of Yeshua, the Messiah of all Israel. Their awakening, recognition, and performance as Ephraim, and their union with Judah, is a necessity for salvation of "all" Israel, and the restoration of the kingdom to Israel (Gen 48:19; Hosea 1:9-10; 5:3; 8:8; Amos 9:9; Jer 31:18-19; Zec 10:7; Rom 9:24-26; 11:26; Eph 2:11-22).

We declare that Yeshua's followers were not meant to replace Judah as Israel, but as "Ephraim," they are part of the called out ones (ekklesia), and in these last-days, the Father is leading them to, whenever scripturally possible, join with Judah; that Judah (faithful Jewish ones who will receive Messiah) and Ephraim (faithful non-Jewish Messiah followers) ultimately will fulfill the destiny of Israel's two houses: that together they might fulfill the prophesies about the one, unified, victorious people of Israel (Jer 31:9; Rom 8:29; Col 1:15,18; 2:12; Heb 12: 22-24; Lev 23:2-36; Exo 19:5; 1 Pet 1:1; 2:9; Jer 3:18; 23:6; Zec 8:13; 12:1-5; Mat 25:31-46; Exo 12:48-49; Num 15:15-16; Isa 56:3,6-8).

We maintain that up to this general time "blindness in part" has happened to all (both houses) of Israel, and as the blinders are lifted, non-Jewish followers in Yeshua will gain insight into their role as Ephraim and become defenders of scriptural Torah and of Judah, and due to this character change, many Jewish people will accept Yeshua as Messiah. This process has begun as indicated through the Messianic Jewish movement (Judah), the Christian Zionism movement (Ephraim), and the Messianic Israel movement (union of Judah and Ephraim) (Isa 8:14; 11:13; Rom 11:25,26; Jer 33:14-16; 31:18-19; Ezek 37:15-28).

The reunion and full restoration of the two houses: This is the hope that burns in the hearts of those of Messianic Israel...

Biography

*B*atya Wootten and her husband, Angus, were early pioneers in the Messianic movement. Decades ago they published the first Messianic materials catalog, created to serve a fledgling new interest in Israel and the Jewish people.

Batya read countless books so she could write book descriptions for the catalogue, and so she discovered the great diversity of opinions about Israel's role and identity.

Hungering to truly understand "Israel," she began to cry out in desperation to her heavenly Father, asking Him to show her *His* truth. As promised, He answered: "Call to Me and I will answer you, and I will tell you great and mighty things, which you do not know" (Jeremiah 33:3).

He began to open up the Scriptures to her, which ultimately led to writing a number of books about Israel, the feasts, and now about the women of Israel.

Batya's books represent decades of study on these crucial issues. Readers have been transformed as they read about all Israel. It is a truth that is helping to restore a long broken brotherhood.

Batya's emphasis on the need to have mercy and grace for both houses is helping to heal the wounds that began when Israel was divided into the Northern Kingdom of Israel and Southern Kingdom of Judah.

Her feast book is said to be the "best," most "liberating,," and most "inspiring" of the books on this subject. And her latest book, *Mama's Torah* is written with a prayer for restoration, for women everywhere, and for her beloved Israel.

Batya is married to her best friend, Col. Angus Wootten (Ret.), author of the visionary book, *Restoring Israel's Kingdom,* plus the handy Commandments guide, *Take Two Tablets Daily*. Together, they have ten children who have blessed them with many heirs.

Angus and Batya developed the informative Messianic Israel web site: *messianicisrael.com*, which in turn led to the founding of the *Messianic Israel Alliance*—a rapidly growing alliance of congregations and home fellowships. This cutting-edge Alliance is now administered by a dedicated Shepherds Council.

They are available for speaking engagements, and they are presently working to publish more books that will minister to the Body of Messiah.

For this assignment they have been uniquely prepared by the God of Abraham, Isaac, and Jacob.

"Let the one who is taught share all good things with him who teaches" (Galatians 6:6).

If through this book a good thing has been accomplished in your life, please write and share your good news with me.

Batya Wootten
PO Box 700217, Saint Cloud, FL 34770
e-mail: batya@mim.net

Who Is Israel? Past, Present, and Future by Batya Ruth Wootten   The scriptural answer to this provocative question is causing a stir in the Body of Messiah. It is sparking a reformation and inspiring Believers everywhere!

Who is Israel? Why do *you* need to know? The way you define Israel sets the course for your interpretation of Scripture. This popular book, now in its third edition, explains the truth about "both the houses of Israel" (Isaiah 8:14)— Ephraim and Judah. Reading it will help you to: Discover your Hebraic Heritage – Understand Israel and the Church – The Father's master plan for Israel. It will explain why you feel something is missing in your life – Why you have a love for Israel and Jewish people – And why you feel an urge to celebrate the feasts of Israel. Includes maps and charts. Paper, 288 pages $14.95 ISBN 1-886987-17-3

Ephraim and Judah: Israel Revealed by Batya Ruth Wootten   Inexpensive. Succinct. Easy-to-read. This condensed overview of the material presented in the classic, *Who Is Israel?,* includes maps, charts, and lists. Like its parent, this book too is encouraging a reformation in the Body of Messiah.   It quickly clarifies misconceptions about Israel's Twelve Tribes. It is an excellent tool that helps non-Jewish Believers see that they too are part of Israel. It also helps both the houses of Israel see how and where they fit into the Father's divine plan (Jeremiah 31:18-19; Ephesians 2:11-22; Isaiah 8:14).

This invaluable handout readily outlines the essence of the phenomenal truth of the two houses of Israel. Paper, 80 pages, $ 3.95   ISBN 1-886987-11-4

Now in Spanish: ¿Quién es Israel? Based on an earlier edition of *Who is Israel?*, this classic is also available in Spanish. 320 pages. $14.95   ISBN 1-886987-08-4

Israel's Feasts and their Fullness by Batya R. Wootten Liberating. Informative. Concise. Written especially for those who understand about both houses of Israel. A well researched, insightful, and highly enjoyable work. Encourages us in the freedom of Messiah, yet shows reverence for the accuracy of Scripture and due respect for Judaism's honorable truths. Addresses Shabbat and the seven feasts of Israel. Includes "Instruction Guides" for the Sabbath, Havdalah, and Passover, plus numerous charts, tables, and graphics. Batya continues in the style that has endeared her to so many readers, as she invites us to dance and sing and celebrate in the presence of the Almighty! Paper, 384 pages, $17.95   ISBN 1-886987-02-5

Passover in all its Fullness Offers the Passover related chapters from the above Feast book, plus helpful Passover Instruction Guides and traditional Messianic Jewish Pesach Haggadah. Explains the Four Passovers of Scripture, the meaning of First Fruits. An ideal gift at Passover celebrations. 96 pages, $4.95   ISBN 1-886987-15-7

Mama's Torah: The Role of Women by Batya Ruth Wootten The fresh ideas offered in this book about the restoration of women and Israel are compelling. Explains the God-ordained role of woman. Defines what it means to be a "help meet." Explains why women sometimes seem to be "against" their husbands. Delightfully depicts the roles of husband and wife. Lists women of the Old and New Covenants and defines *how* they were used. Addresses Scriptures that have traditionally been used to hinder women in their walk. Reveals the Father's call to women in this hour. Includes many study helps. Paper, 144 pages, $9.95   ISBN 1-886987-20-3

Restoring Israel's Kingdom by Angus Wootten   As they stood on the Mount of Olives, the last question Yeshua's disciples asked of Him was, *"Lord, is it at this time You are restoring the kingdom to Israel?"* (Acts 1:6).

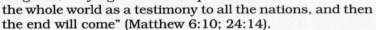

Yeshua told us to pray,"Your kingdom come. Your will be done, on earth as it is in heaven." He proclaimed "the gospel of the kingdom," saying it must be "preached in the whole world as a testimony to all the nations, and then the end will come" (Matthew 6:10; 24:14).

Have we lost sight of the vision that once burned in the hearts of His first disciples? Do we truly understand the Gospel? Do we have the same goal as that of the Messiah of Israel? This inspiring book will help you to keep your eye on the goal. Chapters include: Are You Prepared? – Learning the Lessons of History – Who is a Jew? A Look at Israel's Bloodline – The Way of the Gentiles – Ephraim, Once Again a Mighty Man – The Jubilee Generation – Restoring The Kingdom To Israel – The Messianic Vision – When Will Yeshua Return? – Preparing For The Final Battle. Paper, 304 pages, $14.95   ISBN 1-886987-04-1

Take Two Tablets Daily: The 10 Commandments and 613 Laws by Angus Wootten Shows the laws of Moses to be instructions given to help Israel be strong, courageous, healthy, and blessed.

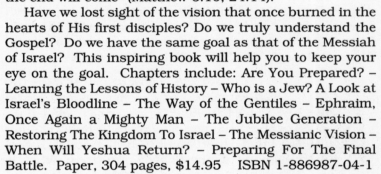

This handy guide lists the 613 laws, divided into Mandatory Commandments and Prohibitions (according to Jewish custom). It also gives the Scripture verse(s) from which each law is derived.

YHVH's Word is like medicinal ointment, and nothing is more symbolic of His Word than the two tablets on which He wrote His desires for us. Taken daily, these "Two Tablets" will give us life more abundantly. This reference book should be in every Believers library. It is a must read. 96 pages, $4.95   ISBN1-886987-06-8

Return to the Land: An Ephraimite's Journey Home by Ephraim Frank As a new Believer, Ephraim could not explain what he felt burning in his soul. He only knew that he was being drawn, wooed by His God, and that he had gone on a tour that had forever changed his life...

From the farm lands of America to the Holy Land of Israel, this compelling autobiography tells of a "stranger" who felt divinely drawn to both the Promised Land and the God of Abraham, Isaac, and Jacob. It tells of the birthing of a new and fresh move of the Holy One, while it gently reveals what the Father is doing in the earth today. It tells of the blessed redemption of the whole house of Israel. Paper, 240 pages, $12.95   ISBN 1-886987-18-1

One Nation Under God by Crystal Lenhart   Good News for our Children! This illustrated and fun book is written on a fifth grade level, to help you share your faith with your children. (Also helps parents better understand Israel.) Use this tool to teach your children in a family-oriented Bible study. Great for home schooling and elementary adult studies. Features pages to color, lots of graphics, maps and illustrations, plus easily understood lesson overviews and summaries.

Crystal writes, "The Bible speaks of one nation that was designed to be an example for all other nations. In Psalm 147, the Psalmist tells us that only this nation has been given God's Words and ordinances. The apostle Paul writes in Ephesians that every New Covenant Believer gains citizenship in this nation. What is this nation of the Bible? You guessed it, ISRAEL! Israel is Yahveh's nation, created to be a great nation with wise and understanding people, with a God who dwells among them and who has given them righteous laws to live by." Paper, Spiral Bound, 8x11, 76 pages, $12.00 ISBN 1-886987-16-5

Unlocking *your* future...

Distributed by:

Messianic
Israel
Ministries

PO Box 3263
Lebanon, TN
37088

1 800 829-8777
www.mim.net

Notes

Notes